Autism:

The Way We Look At It

Freda McEwen

Autism: The Way We Look At It

Copyright © 2016 FREDA MCEWEN

ISBN 978-1533612441

Carerswecare4 Ltd

carerswecareltd@gmail.com

Sidney Sanni Publishing London

ACKNOWLEDGEMENT

I am grateful to God for the good health and well-being that were necessary to complete this book.

I will always be ever thankful to my mother Madam Esther Ozueh and late father Fred McEwen for raising me up as a confident and hardworking woman. My mum taught me, the value of hard work and my dad, self-denial. And my appreciation goes to the blessed children Tony Abara and Tochi Abara, the reward God has given me, without them I would not have reached this level. And my gratefulness to God for giving me siblings who have been an added value to my life, Shola Chigbo, Late Umaru Altine, Moina Umaru Altine and Late Fred McEwen my twin brother And to all my friends who have always been there for me particularly, Prince Bola Adebayo, Pastor and Mrs Enemou, Mr and Mrs Okeke, Pastor and Mrs Sanni. And my dear friends who have taken out time to read and edit this book Ajibola Egbedeyi and Dr Uzoma Odenigbo

-

Table of contents

INTRODUCTION

BEING TONY'S MUM

This is a life journey I took with no desire for pessimism.

It does get gloomy sometimes and I do get moody just like every human. I had to be optimistic and take every step in affirmation that it would get better. There are times that I had to be woken up by life's idealism and embittered by (supposedly) Autism parading itself like a miniature god.

All in all, I have made life choices to be strong, realising that the world is waiting to unveil Tony's destiny and I have been given the responsibility to ensure that his destiny is not thwarted by events of life. I have nurtured him in full submission to nature's expectations. I am glad that autism is not attributed to nurture but nature, otherwise I would have been living in dilemma and self blame.

As you read my journey, you will understand that I am just an act within the script of life. I can only play my part by ensuring that Tony - the major character - is in line as scripted and you the spectators are satisfied.

Letter to parents of children with Autism

Dear beloved,

I am writing this to assure you that you are not on your own. We parents of children with autism have diversified experiences. The most compelling thing is how we all deal with it. Some children may seem better than the other due to having life skills but behind closed doors there are more disheartening stories to tell. There are others whose children have no life skills or limited life skills but are very passive and less chaotic. And others likewise expose their parents to traumatic experiences. In all these I must affirm that life is never worriless but worrisome. Do not be perturbed by the outward disguise of accomplishment and content in people who fake everything about their existence – it is all facade. Please be encouraged as life has provided you with an inner ability to survive. There is an inner strength which life has deposited inside of you and that is why you have been given privilege to parent a special child. I love you my friend and I hope you get all your answers from my experiences. I wish I can reach out and hug you, but unfortunately not, but my heart is with you and I can assure you that this book is packaged with heartfelt messages and testimonies. I wish you all your heart desire. Hang in there! I can see a light at the end of the dark tunnel and a hand aiding your passage.

My dear friend, we have all come thru thus far so what new challenges can overcome us?

We are over comers and victors packaged delicately and unassumingly, humiliating all life terrors. We may be challenged but we channel all life distractions to an exit point of no return.

Love you lot. xxxx

CHAPTER 1

Birth

When babies are born, the first thing they do is wail. They wail and wail until they become too tired for their tiny bodies to bear. Birth seems like a very strange phenomenon. It accentuates the pain felt by both parties—mother and baby. Being born into this world is a painful process accompanied by uncertainties. The baby is unsure of what to expect from the world, and the world on the other hand is anxious and expectant. Life is too complex with so much to unravel, yet no one has ever had the slightest clue of what it holds. Birth involves a sequence of celebration, the aftermath BEING a cuddly angelic inheritance. Birth is a cord-breaking process where the child is detached from the mother's womb. Outside the labour room is festive with gallons of booze, popping champagne, lighting cigars, decorating the home, and lots of high calorie mouth-watering food for entertainment. Whilst mum is still recovering from the birth incident and the cuts from the baby passage, the baby is still wrapped up in mucus and blood, waiting to be checked to ensure there are no birth defects. It is like a journey with an unknown outcome in that not everyone that enters the labour room comes out alive. Some women die in the process and others fall very ill or even go into coma or become paralysed.

There is doubt in expecting that life drama will always turn out as staged or scripted. The author gives us the liberty to make our role as we choose either to mimic the author's script or to adjust it to our desire. Sometimes, we get it all wrong and by the time we make a U-turn to learn our role as scripted, we totally miss the entire event and end up helpless.

I will tell you my story from the moment I walked into the hospital to report swelling in my arms and leg. I told the doctor I needed an ultrasound but she said it was not necessary. I put my foot down and told her I did not think the swelling was a good sign. Reluctantly, she agreed that I could have ultrasound. It is very important that everyone educate themselves on any ailment that they are going through. Pregnant women especially, need to read extensively to understand the duties medical practitioners owe -them and what their rights are. It is your life after all, so you should endeavour to protect it through knowledge. As the saying goes, 'knowledge is power'.

My ultrasound result showed that I did not have water enough in my womb. My doctor panicked and got me into the labour room immediately to break the water. Oh dear, it was such a painful process but thankfully, I soon recovered from it. My nightmare, however, began from this point on. I was given medication to assist me with contraction but despite the medication, I was in labour for three days and finally had a caesarian section as my cervix was unable to dilate. This is not too good medically. Oops, they messed up.

During my antenatal consultations, doctors had noticed that I had strep B, a form of bacteria found in a third of pregnant women. It is not a sexually transmitted infection and it causes no symptoms, it is found in the vagina, however, it can be transmitted from a mother to an unborn child during labour and can cause a serious illness known as Group B Strep infection disease.

I am not a medical practitioner but breaking the water in my womb and allowing me to be in labour for days was a case of serious negligence, coupled with the fact that I had strep B. Well, due to ignorance, I did not charge the hospital for their negligence or seek prosecution even though I was in the land of litigation—the USA.

I also developed Bell's palsy during the last trimester of my pregnancy, which is a paralysis or weakness of the muscles on one side of the face. Damage to the facial nerve that controls muscles on one side of the face causes that side of the face to droop. The nerve damage may also affect a person's sense of taste and the control of tears and saliva. This condition comes on suddenly, often overnight, and usually gets better on its own within a few weeks. I am not sure why I developed the Bell's palsy but my sister had taken me to relax my hair using a chemical-based relaxer the day before so I wondered if that was the cause.

I also developed severe preeclampsia. Women and babies die or get very sick each year from a dangerous condition called pre-eclampsia, a life-threatening disorder that occurs only during pregnancy and the post-partum period. Pre-eclampsia is most often characterized by a rapid rise in blood pressure that can lead to seizure, stroke, multiple organ failure, or death of the mother and/or baby.

As if this pain was not enough, another surprise sprang up whilst my stitches was being removed. The scar opened up. My God! I exclaimed. 'What wrong did I do? Perhaps my existence or having a child was an offence to some people.' I reminded myself that 'He that is in me is greater than he that is in the world'. I am the apple of God's eyes and the thoughts He has for me are of good and not evil to bring me to an expected end.

This was my labour experience, my first pregnancy for that matter. Why I went through all these, I am not sure but I know that the one who created me and my son has a divine purpose and reason for everything. He intervened, every step of the way.

One afternoon, I was lying in a cosy single bed en suite hospital room when a nurse walked into the room. She was white, blonde and in her early thirties. She came and sat next to me on the bed, hugged me, then looked into my eyes with so much compassion and whispered to me in a quiet and soothing unearthly voice, 'Freda, I'm sure you are wondering if God has left you. He hasn't, He is right here with you and will give you complete healing. If you need anything, call this number.' She inscribed something in a book I was reading and left. I never saw her again. I called her 'Angel' and still call her Angel. Her coming that day brought me and my baby hope. It lifted my spirit to another level of hope and enthusiasm.

Though I hurt and I go through countless pains and tribulations, still something inside me springs forth hope and assurance that my redeemer lives and cares for me a zillion times. He loves me more than life. My situation has equipped me to become a shock absorber, able to divert every fiery dart of the enemy. I know days of fretting are over, and I am about to embark on something impossible—my ministry unleashed by my enemies unknowingly.

CHAPTER 2

Motherhood

Now I will go back to introduce the star of this book—Tony. When Tony was born, he was not breathing and he did not cry because he was tired from prolonged labour. My baby was on oxygen in the intensive care unit to aid his breathing. I was wheeled in the wheelchair to see him and carry him when I needed to. My experience was very odd. I was too weak to breastfeed my baby so he had formula all through.

I was perplexed and confused by the whole issue but it did not rewrite or unmake the works the creator had started in my life. Holding the creature I was blessed with, made me excited and I wished for a second I could wrap my arms around him and whisper with so much intensity 'I love you, son'. But he was too delicate to feel such overpowering warmth. Handsome delicate features made me wonder if he came from me. He was gorgeous. A heavenly sent treasure packaged in such a delicate fascinating parcel. I would say he is a covenant child, a priceless blessing and a glorious gift. Every child is a blessing from the creator of the universe, a gift from his bosom. I love him to bits and till date, I call him MUMMY'S BLESSING. I will not exchange him for another regardless of their cognitive and intellectual ability. I have not given up yet on what my maker has in store for

Tony. It might take time but I will surely wait for it.

Tony developed normally and reached set milestones as medical practitioners had predicted. Mother's instinct though, I knew there was something not quite right. Tony was passive, very quiet, and used his hand gestures in an extraordinarily abnormal manner. He did not crawl but started walking at 15 months. He had few words and enjoyed playing on his own flapping his hands. He never paid any attention to teddy bears or other toys. At about 18 months, I noticed some changes after the MMR injection—the alleged cause of autism. To be candid, I would say that children diagnosed with autism after MMR are already susceptible due to one birth defect or the other. More so, at 18 months, it is easier for a parent to notice developmental changes in a child compared to when they are younger.

I must say that every one of us have a distinctive coping mechanism which enables us to cope more than most. Mine emanates from my belief and that is why I dedicated my son to spiritual service and purity prior to having the knowledge of his diagnosis. I did not do that out of desperation as I was young and agile with no concerns but in full acclamation that he is my first fruit of the womb.

Tony developed nicely without any form of medical condition; he slept well and ate like a giant. At the age of 4, he ate 4 weetabix and hot chocolate for breakfast. One day, my landlady who was quite friendly pulled me aside to advise me that I should take my son to the GP that his behaviour seemed rather odd. I asked her what she meant by odd and she gave me instances of children diagnosed with autism. I did not know what that ailment meant so I went to the library, read books, asked friends, neighbours, nutritionists, and spoke to my health visitor. My health visitor was not convinced my son had any problem, she felt it was a figment of my imagination. All the nutritionist had to say was that I should stop Tony's Weetabix and hot chocolate breakfast as they were detrimental to his health and would make him hyperactive. Tony's dad also felt I was putting an unnecessary tag on him—he was living in self-denial. As for me, I needed a quick fix to revamp any prognosis.

At this stage, it was as if the world was suddenly shutting down, my relationship was breaking down and I was torn between two emotions—my child or my relationship. I knew I owed my innocent child a lot. His dad was an adult, old enough to handle any situation. I cried in my sleep, I talked to myself and God mostly, because no human understood what was happening within me but God. To add to the complexity, I got pregnant again and had a little girl. My hormones were out of control but God was in control. I encouraged myself in the only one I know and can rely on— 'the Holy Spirit'. I knew at this point that I had to lean on the Father of wisdom and comforter, and he did exactly that, he showed me the way forward. Tony became withdrawn, transfixed, and was always busy kissing his baby sister's hands. He was always admiring her and lying beside her. Guess what! Things have changed now, they are both adults-Every man for himself. Unfortunately things have changed between them as Tony finds it difficult to comprehend why I should share my motherly affection with his sister. He cries sometimes when his sister comes to me. Oh, well I cannot push my daughter aside, even though she is 18 years old now, she still needs her mum. I am beginning to work with Tony to appreciate that his sister needs me as much as he does. He also started bossing everyone in the house around, trying to tell us to sit down when we stand up, on my own part I am trying to stand firm and tell him, I am the mother and I give orders. Thank God, he fully understood me and backed off-well done Freda!!!!!

CHAPTER 3

Tony's Speech is Gone

I suddenly stopped hearing my baby say those single words around the age of 18 months. He was not even responding to his name or any word spoken to him. I noticed that he was not focusing, no single eye contact. He was oblivious of his surrounding and was locked up in a world of his own, which I called 'spellbound', mesmerised, or transfixed into something. I was unable to comprehend what was happening. What is this autism? I understood it to be a personality manipulating my child's life. I saw it as a stranger in my house harassing and tormenting my child's existence. I perceived autism as 'bogus' or perhaps a demon, an imaginary nasty personality dominating my child's mood negatively. No matter what I assumed this autism was, it became a terror that repeatedly brought tears to my eyes. This evil has disrupted households, caused marital breakdown, ill health, joblessness, financial crisis, social isolation, and terminal diseases. I had to apologise for my son's disability, I even said sorry without reason just to apologise for the future things my son might do like step on people, snatch people's food at restaurants, pick things from trolleys, lay on shop floor screaming and the most depressing one is a 10-year-old doing a poo in his nappy.

Autism scars most households it enters into, and leaves an indelible mark which I believe can be permanently erased only by the inner strength given to every loving and caring parent at the creation and conception process. All we need to do is reunite with it. The victim is isolated and the ailment tagged as a taboo for the ignorant, and sometimes perceived as contagious. People look at the victim as if they are alien; and to their family, as if they have inherited a curse. I stopped visiting friends and families apart from those who understood the condition and were less judgemental.

Truly speaking, no one has a clue about this autism but we all rely on some definitions medical practitioners, researchers, and psychologists come up with. Sometimes there are some spiritual interpretations by some primitive barbaric societies who mutilate and create physical pains in these children with autism, with the assumption that they are possessed by an evil spirit or perhaps witchcraft.

My son was locked up in this illusion that never seemed to end. No matter how I enticed him, he was disinterested in anything surrounding him. It was more like we were mere objects; he focused more on designs in my clothing than in me. When I came back from shopping, he was not interested in my arrival but in the food. I was totally perplexed his reaction. My child was no longer affectionate towards me his birth mother; he was consumed by things or objects rather than human beings. It seemed like he stopped recognising who we are or even who he is. I always reminded him, 'you are Tony', 'I am Mummy', and 'this is your sister, Tochi'. He just ignored me as if I was blabbing. He wouldn't answer his name when he was called. Perhaps he was now deaf and dumb, I assumed. I took him to an otolaryngologist or audiologist to look at his ears to see what the problem was. They ran series of tests and told me there was nothing wrong with his ears. I even ran tests ranging from MRI scan, EEG, and blood test to see if he had fragile X, but all the results were negative.

I phoned a very good friend of mine and shared my problem regarding my son's speech. She advised me that I should try various ways to communicate with him using things that he really likes, and ask him to come and take them. As soon as I dropped the phone, I felt like a child who woke up one Christmas morning to discover an unexpected present from Santa. I jumped at this new idea and put it into action immediately. Tony was upstairs in his room watching cartoon with his sister and I called his name twice but he did not answer. I called him again, this time I told him to come and take. In less than a minute, my son was flying downstairs and looking at my empty hand as if to say 'so where is the stuff then?' I was happy to at least know he was not deaf. I was flabbergasted and so excited; I took him and his sister to McDonalds to celebrate, a battle just won.. It was wonderful to know that my son could both speak and hear. My dear friend I started at that point to encourage him to speak. I knew he knows how to help himself round the house without communicating his needs but I refused to encourage self help. I decided to ask him 'What do you want? If he answers Rice, I will insist on him making a full sentence 'I want Rice please and to say thank you when given. I had to plead with his school not to use sign language, lots of visual and vocal aid. I was skeptical that if these were used independently without encouraging speech it can make the child mute. Please do not underestimate your child's ability; every child is able if encouraged unless they are disabled at birth.

I can only thank the one and only who orchestrates the events of life and assures us that total dependence on Him brings security and assurance.

CHAPTER 4

Diagnosis

At 4 years old, Tony was finally diagnosed with autism. It was difficult for the child psychologist to come up with the diagnosis. They needed to give him more time. They suggested it might have been as a result of the relationship breakdown between his dad and me. Parenthood is a major role and we owe a duty to our children to ensure that our emotional issues have no bearing in their thriving. Children are very sensitive, even babies more so, they have a strong attachment to their mothers' particularly male children. Male children from the time of conception have a strong protective bond with their mothers and when she is going through emotional difficulties, it affects them to a great degree. I suppose that is why as the society becomes more reckless and negligent in responding to the needs of parenthood, the more predominant rate of children being diagnosed with autism. It is important that men and women who are not ready to control their emotional outbursts and feelings not to engage themselves in bringing up children without psychological help or counselling. We are living in a very selfish society where people are not bothered by the impact of their behaviour on others. These days we have children taking care of their parents, cleaning them up after a heavy alcohol binge or snorting on drugs, or separating them from physical combat and abusive language war. Who is taking care of whom? If care is not taken, the end time surge as predicted by the bible, will be taking place where parents war against themselves and children against parents. Sometimes I wish I had focused more on the person inside me who is able to bring peace to my entire being—the holy spirit—my comforter and my teacher. Perhaps things would have been different.

I diverted all my energy and ability to get things right for my son but guess what? My strength is not enough and can never be, but total reliance and complete dependence on God can make things better and that is how I get my strength, please find an avenue to off load your stress and emotional concerns. It can be through counselling coaching or exercise.

The day Tony was diagnosed with autism was like a jail sentence for me. I stood before the doctor who was swallowing between her words; it was difficult for her to tell me. She kept asking me, 'are you okay? Are you okay?' 'I am okay,' I said, because He that is in me has built resilience in me to be able to bounce back regardless of any situation. The doctor explained what autism was and it was different from my own perception as an observer.

According to the National Autistic Society, autism is a lifelong developmental disability that affects how a person communicates with and relates to other people. It also affects how they make sense of the world around them.

I met parents who were crying and heartbroken by the news, but my maker kept me strong. I don't need to allow the enemy to celebrate my sadness but I want the enemy to be anxious at my unperturbed mood. My family and friends were very sad at the news, everyone felt it was a phase that will one day disappear, though it never did, I am still celebrating the blessing of having him and the joy it gives me.. I am thankful for the grace to love my son and to believe he will be better one day. Even if things remain the same, it will not change the fact that God is God, and 'He rewards diligence. I started doing research and attending courses on how to improve my child's life. I read up on and attended lectures, seminars and workshops like; the SONRISE program: A home-based parent-directed, relationship-based play therapy program for children with autistic spectrum disorder and other developmental disabilities. The program was developed by Barry Neil Kaufman and Samahria Lyte Kaufman for their autistic son, who was claimed to have fully recovered from his condition. (Wikipedia free encyclopedia)

LOVAAS program: The Lovaas model is a form of Early Intensive Behavioral Intervention (EIBI) developed by Psychology Professor Dr Ivar Lovaas at the University of California, Los Angeles (UCLA). Using the science of Applied Behavior Analysis (ABA), the technique is carried out early in the development of autistic and developmentally-delayed children, and is the only therapy to have gone under approval by the United States Surgeon General's office in 1999. It involves discrete-trial teaching, breaking skills down into their most basic components, rewarding positive performance with praise and reinforcement, and then 'generalizing' skills in a naturalistic setting. (Wikipedia free encyclopedia)

My son also went to school full time, but it was difficult to assure continuity especially when the school method contradicted what I was teaching at home. I was finding it difficult to balance both. Tony started doing very well spelling his name, counting up to a hundred, reading back story books and using the computer. This was in primary school but in secondary school year nine, things took a very negative turn. My son reverted to where he was years ago. I will discuss this issue further in subsequent chapters.

My son's disability did not hold me down; instead it has moved me to achieve my heart's desire. It spurred me into being more ambitious and working towards the last hierarchy of needs by Abraham Maslow—self-actualisation. .

Stagnation is for the weak-minded and those who have decided to allow their inadequacies and experiences to determine their move or those who have decided to rely on their own strength. For those who choose to rely on God's promise to meet them at the point of their needs, He will embed in them the ability to do exploits and remain progressive.

Life issues are there to strengthen us and move us to heights. Do not ponder on what your issues are, but what you desire to be. Issues do not determine us; we divert them to focus on who is in us. And He that is in us is greater than the greatest that is in the world. The whole earth and all that is in it belongs to the creator of the universe and all, and they freeze at His presence he knows my name and when and where I am and will be going.

CHAPTER 5

Toilet Game

This chapter will spur me into going into phases of ISMS within the Autistic Spectrum Disorder which are patterns of behaviours. I would advise you, if your system is weak, don't eat before reading it or perhaps don't eat while reading it. This chapter I call the toilet game.

As you can imagine, children with autism pick up habits and drop them, some of which are dangerous and painful. I hated every minute of this phase. One day, I was giving my son a shower when he was about 10 years old. I went to my room to pick up the towel. When I came back I noticed something brownish in the bath tub smeared all over the bathroom tiles. It was not dirt . . . it was poo. It cannot possibly be dirt, because I am 'Miss Clean'. My friends and family call me that, and some even say 'maybe she has obsessive compulsive disorder (OCD)'. People in the world use this phrase 'cleanliness is next to Godliness' so I believe that being dirty and unkempt is ungodly (LOL). That is my casual comment if you are not so modern it means *laugh out loud*. I bleached and bleached my bath tub and tiles all the time under normal circumstance, so you can imagine what happened after this incident. A whole tub of bleach! I lay down and cried not out of self-pity but confusion as to why this was happening. I picked up myself quickly. The wonderful caring companion inside me, 'the Holy Spirit', poured an oil of gladness all over me with the assurance that everything has a solution and there is nothing new under the sun.

I washed my beloved son, cleaned the bath tub and carried on with normal chore as if nothing happened. Sweetheart, I did not seek human support, I sought the supernatural that is able and available.

Toilet issues baffle parents with children with autism they don't seem to comprehend how these children come up with some scary habits and yet they are very healthy. Some families complain about these children eating their poo and constantly smearing them on the bedroom walls. It is very disturbing and petrifying to observe a child come up with such inhumane habit. Some researches have come up with the findings that these children have sensory issues. All these are mere speculations and none conclusive yet so many carers are psychologically, mentally and emotionally tortured by observing these incidence. My heart bleeds and goes out to children and parents with children who face this kind of traumatic experience over a very long period of time, thank goodness mine did not last up to 3 episodes. What took a toll on me was Tony pooing inside the bath tub, as this lasted for 3 months, it became a nightmare and I started being strict on him and telling him off then not long he stopped. As soon as he got potty trained he stopped, it is difficult potty training a child with autism especially boys, but all hope is not lost if I can potty train mine, anyone can. It is about prioritising and ensuring they are potty trained before the age of 3 years old.

If you are reading this book I pray for you that your experience shall and will be no more in Jesus name. If you are not a parent please take out time just a minute and seek God's face for this children and family.

Autism is like a package sent to affected families wrapped severally with unending wrap. It takes time to unravel the content as knowledgeable and wise you maybe you can never suss it. Every package is different with diversifying heartbreaking experiences.

These habits can be very costly as well as unhealthy. Money is spent buying toilet rolls that have been eaten on a daily basis. Some block the toilet and sink and even cause flooding whilst others run the water and electricity constantly. These habits not only leave you bemused but leak your pocket. I met a lady whose 16 years old son is still not potty trained, he smears poo on a regular basis. Her son goes to an expensive school for children with Autism paid by the state, in this instance the school is used as a premise for care rather than education which is wrong. This lady became ill from her caring role, what is important at this stage? Do our children get into institutions as a tick box exercise or statistical purposes or monetary gain? What is important for this child is potty training; this will save tax payers money if one important area is targeted, rather than none, meanwhile someone is getting paid for nothing. Social workers should be doing proper risk assessment to ascertain the way forward for their client. ?   Our children are weird, people say, but we know that they are special. Some would say they hear inner voices that ask them to do inappropriate things? Shall we then come to the conclusion that they lack the ability to control the inner negative voices? We all so called normal people sometimes have an inner thought to do something very weird but we don't. Sometimes you have these inner feeling to slap someone who offended you but you don't or even say something very awkward but you don't. This is because you have control over your inner thought and the ability to retain, delete and filter information. People with autism lack diplomacy they can't read between the lines or see beyond black and white.

What is normal I often question, who gives prognosis of normality or abnormality? Who indeed is normal these days, perhaps none as most people these days belong to the spectrum?

Man has tendency to feel sorry for you and sometimes makes you feel worse. They are volatile in nature and you don't know what to expect, so I will not advise you to try. But God is constant; He will never ever let you down. He can never be too busy to attend to your needs, He is the omnipresence.

All done for that day, the next day, he repeated the same thing and this kept happening over and over again repeatedly, and I kept bleaching and bleaching the bath tub. One day, something inside me said to me *he is human, if you can train a dog, you can do that with human. He is still a child and you can tell him not do that again.* The next day when he did the same thing, I looked sternly at him. Pointing at the poo, I said, 'Mummy is not happy, that is very naughty, Tony. Do not do that again, it's very bad.' He looked at me and I could see he felt bad that he did it. I then spoke to him in a gentle simple manner without agitating him. Since then he stopped doing it.

Tony was quite conscious of my facial expressions and moods. Thank God I don't have mood swings otherwise I would have swung him into additional problem. If you have mood swings and you have children with psychological, emotional, or mental disorder, please seek help or you will worsen the situation. Perhaps you may try to make a little effort to control your mood, which could be achievable through selflessness.

I forgot to explain to you how Tony regained his eye contact. After the SONRISE program, I learnt how to give and get eye contact. At that stage, my son was reading my lips and not making eye contact. I started by copying his actions. When he flapped his hands, I did the same; when he jumped, I jumped. To be able to communicate effectively with a person with autism, you need to invite yourself to their world by doing what they do without condemning them. Let them see themselves from your image. When I copied him, he stopped and started laughing. That was how communication was introduced. When I spoke to him, I ensured he made eye contact with me. Eye contact helps to facilitate communication. Most autistic children hate speaking just as much as they hate some sounds. If you don't assist a child with autism to expand their vocabulary, they can grow mute. Enforce communication through asking them to express themselves more in order to get what they want. They need to know that language is power and can help you to get what you want.

My son liked using single words like 'drink', 'sleep', 'eat', 'toilet'. I always pretended not to understand and always said to him 'what do you want?' He then went on to say what he wanted—'I want rice, please' or 'I want black currant please'.

Well my son was still in nappies at 10 years old. It was a nightmare putting incontinence large nappies on him. I was praying and wishing this nightmare will be over. Yes, it was over when I met a young man who assisted me in potty training him, and a child minder who was eager to get him off nappy. God intervened by using these people. Everyone in our life has a role to play and it is important that we pray that God will give us the insight as to what their roles are; thank God I latched onto that. I called this the toilet game because during this period, I experienced a lot of toilet games. Now my son decided to wash his hands in the toilet. I don't mean the sink, but the toilet. I just could not comprehend why he did that when there was a sink right in front of him. He started eating tissues and spitting them back in the toilet. Oh my God!!! It was unbecomingly ridiculous; I could not fathom how someone will come up with such dangerous habit. I am fascinated by the fact that the maker has inscribed in this young man's life grace, mercy, and love and that is what keeps him going regardless of all the tantrums from the devil and his cohorts.

Like I mentioned in a previous chapter, I made a covenant with God, and He kept Tony safe regardless of the enemy's manipulation. I suppose you are wondering if I let him do that unattended, of course not. I watch him whilst in the toilet and when I am distracted for a second he does what he needed to do. My son has an eagle eye and very quick to action. That is why till date my eyes are always alert watching his every move but sometimes I miss it. Remember I said I have a PHD in Autism—just kidding. I had to stop him from eating tissue. I decided to remove tissue from the toilet, and only provided it when Tony was in the toilet and needed tissue. It was a bit of running up and down, but I loved it! I didn't need to pay for the gym as Tony had already provided a physical activity of running up and down the internal stairs.

Just thinking like Tony:

I am Tony, living in my own beautiful sweet world.

I enjoy my company and find other people as interesting poetic stanzas that captivate my entire being.

I study their moods and behaviour.

I gaze at the beautiful pictures on their clothing because they bring alive nature in its artistic manner.

I am fascinated by paintings on their faces and the hairstyles. I stare at people sometimes not because

I want to make friends with them but because the physical features in their faces are all so unique and none seems identical.

Yet they are faces. They range from small to big sizes and their statures fascinate me.

I do not understand or care about beauty but I respond more to the inner beauty which I find very adorable.

I don't have people I call friends. Neither has anyone visited and said they are looking for me.

Apart from my carers, some of them are annoying because they want to force me to take special interest in them.

Some of them are old enough to be my parents and I have one that is close to my age.

I like him and I know he does not see me as just helpless but a buddy. I get away with stuff with him, he lets me muck about sometimes, unlike the rest that almost handcuff me and watch me with so much anxiety.

They say I am a teenager now but nothing seems different except that I feel different inside me.

I love eating; it makes me comfortable and less anxious.

I love sleeping when I am tired but sometimes I am encouraged to sleep even when I am not tired.

I watch my mum and sister fall asleep anywhere, anyhow, and I wonder how they do it.

Like I said, every face is the same and everyone is unique but my mum and sister are special.

I don't understand how I came to exist or where my mum and sister came from.

But all I know is that we all live in the same house and they show me lots of love and attention.

I love my home; it is a place for safety for me.

I haven't been opportune to spend much time away from my mum and sister but I know I love my home.

Sometimes people gaze at me differently and when my mum's eye catches them, they withdraw.

My mum is like a soldier ant, she stings when she needs to protect me.

She is also like mother hen; she builds a nest around me and my sister and fusses over us in an overly protective manner.

My mum is calm, she hates making me or seeing me agitated so I control myself whenever mum is around because I want to keep her sweet.

My mum always says she loves me, I don't understand what that word means but it sounds like a good word.

I said that to mum once and she made so much fuss about it, as if she won a lottery not knowing I was just echolalia, just mere repeating words, I mean just doing what people diagnosed with autism do sometimes.

When mum goes out, I do miss her company but when she comes back, I am only attracted by the food shopping that she brings back.

I don't understand the concept of time as to how long she has been away but her coming home is good.

I enjoy cartoons. They are very creative and interesting to watch, you never get bored.

I hate seeing people on TV because their voices echo back to me as if they are blabbing, not making coherent language.

It's not that I have language or interested in expanding my vocabulary.

I love going on the school bus because it moves and I get to see things around.

As for the passengers, they are the least of my concern provided they do not speak to me.

I don't like what school is, it is more like a joker's paradise. We are all lined up like misfits waiting to be fitted.

Nothing seems normal and nothing looks able, we are disabled with people holding our hands as if we are toddlers.

CHAPTER 6

Hitting Knuckles and Chewing Sleeves

Tony progressed to another habit of hitting his knuckles on hard surfaces and coming up with bruises. This was not a very nice sight; it was what my grandmother would classify as an eyesore. I used to think it was a colloquial expression only to find out online it meant 'hurting the eyes to look at or ugly to the sight'. I prayed and hoped I would open my eyes and Tony's cracked knuckles will be fixed. Well, I did wake up to more bruises on his knuckles. This does not mean that prayer does not work, but perhaps the habit needed to go through its course. Just kidding; the reason I know best is that most things in life cannot be explained on earth. Perhaps we will understand when we all go to the other side of existence—death. After six months, Tony stopped knuckles hitting.

It is difficult for me to explain what those knuckles hitting did to me. It was like a stab to my chest. Sometimes I wondered if they were painful or not, especially as the threshold of pain in children with autism is quite high.

Each tab of his knuckles on the wall penetrated into my bone marrows, but he was oblivious of this. A mother's attachment is very powerful and I would express my feelings like this;

Sometimes I feel life is full of strange happenings

Some you do understand, most you don't

Most of your personal issues are personal

You are the only one that understands how you feel and what you are going through.

People might pity you or perhaps think they empathise

You are the only one that knows what you are facing

The face of the pain is as ugly as you paint the picture

Attentions are drawn to the pictures only to who you care to share though no one could visualise your concept of the true meaning of the picture.

But as someone who cares to care because you care, you will understand and accept the responsibility which life has thrown in your lap and you need to cuddle it and ensure it is safeguarded without questioning.

What questions can you ask or would you ask?

I am personally convinced, resilient and confident enough to know that my love cannot be equated to a common embryonic attachment

But more of an attachment by nature as God ordained it to be.

Perhaps you are reading this and you feel that you have given up on life.

Nothing is too late provided you are still breathing.

You can always dust your shoes and take a step inside to find out the true meaning of life.

Life is for living

Only people who understand live it in full

I am not talking about excessiveness of life like heavy drinking, gluttony and other reckless acts.

But of those who know their God and are listed to do exploits.

I have come to acknowledge and accept of my role in caring for my son. It is an unthankful role but very rewarding. The person may not want to be cared for but you have to. The person may not want physical contact but you have to try. The person might even become violent and abusive, but yet you find ways to cope. The person may not show any emotions but you have to. It might cost you pain and constant discouragement but when you have a will there is always a way. It is unlike most disabilities, much internalised but absolutely commendable. The all knowing that I and you know, the supreme one and creator of US mankind, never allows us to carry what we cannot overcome. I believe we all have a way to deal with our situation without going insane or costing us our life and health. If you are in this situation please latch onto this revelation and claim your sanity

Now my baby moved from hitting knuckles into chewing his sleeves. That was a very expensive habit as he destroyed most of his shirts with sleeves. I stopped putting long sleeve on him and moved to short sleeve. The first day he came back without a chewed sleeve I was so ecstatic that the expensive habit was over. Alas, he came back the second day, and his collar was chewed. *Hmmmmmmm*, Tony is something else, he is so clever. Well, I am mum and have all the knowledge so a toddler should not dictate to me. I went shopping and bought lots of T-shirts and Tony stopped chewing any part of the clothing. I wonder why he did not decide to bite on the other parts of the T-shirt. I thought about it and noticed that Tony did not like the texture of T-shirts; he preferred the cotton shirt type. I might not be a specialist in autism but mother's instinct is the highest PhD. This could be a sensory issue with autism.

Many people within the Autistic Spectrum Disorder (ASD) have difficulty processing everyday sensory information such as sounds, sights, and smells. This is usually called having sensory integration difficulties or sensory sensitivity. It can have a profound effect on a person's life. Children or people with sensory needs are more likely to have behavioural problems as a result of their brain's inability to process these feelings.

I will give you a little story of my childhood. I used to suck on my tongue and lips whilst touching a particular texture of clothing which my brain processes as a solution to most of my needs. It put me to sleep and satisfied my hunger. Yet I developed normally without diagnosis of autism. I also used to bang my head on the bed as a toddler, yet I was not diagnosed with autism. We are living in a generation where labelling is so hugely overrated. Every child is monitored closely not with concern for their well-being but with the sole investigation of seeking to find out something out of the ordinary. That is why most people are inquisitive as to why Autism was not known or diagnosed over 30 years ago, could the answer lie in the modern technology or does it mean man has grown to be more curious, nosey and picky about anything extraordinary. Is life demands becoming too exasperating that people are struggling to catch their breath in-between commitments or are marital demands becoming too unbearable and households are becoming very chaotic.

When I was growing up at school people used words like 'DUNCE 'DULLARD' yet the so called dunce are not 'labelled' but integrated to learn with the rest of 'the student with intelligence and acumen '. They acquired social skills and allowed to thrive in a normal environment without segregation. How come after 60 years people who have lived normal existence are being diagnosed. Are we living in a society where we cuddle up to self pity and worthlessness? We are preoccupied with constant recap of horrific regretful past events of life without letting go. Pardon me, my dear friend I would encourage you to see your child as normal but don't be in self denial. Please be mindful that there are children whose birth circumstances have exposed them to defects, these should not be ignored but helped, not just managed but encouraged to move forward and acquire life skills. Remember everything on earth with life has ability to acquire skills, even your household pet, more so your child.

CHAPTER 7

Chewing Pencils and Indoor Plants

I thought habit phases were over! I decided to buy my son pencils to start colouring and drawing. Every parent would want their child to attain a cognitive progression undoubtedly. I will give him paper and crayon to paint, and by the time I went to the kitchen and back in less than two minutes, he would have chewed on the pencil. I initially felt perhaps the pencil tip was breaking, so I would sharpen it and give it back. One day, I grabbed him gently, opened his mouth and noticed chewed pencil in his mouth. I washed his mouth, cleaned him out, and used lots of water to flush him. I was, so scared, of lead poisoning as pencil is made of lead. I panicked and did various researches on lead, not on pencils. The more I read on lead, the more I panicked. I took him to the GP who told me that pencil lead is actually graphite, and it is not possible to get lead poisoning from it.

Lead poisoning is when damaging or lethal amounts of lead (a very dense heavy metal) enter the bloodstream, causing brain damage and possibly cardiac failure. I was glad that my son would not get lead poisoning, but I still stopped giving him pencils as I was not fully convinced that deposits of that graphite in his system could not be harmful. Sometimes we get paranoid about minor things but forget about more concerning issues like water pipes which are more prevalent in lead poisoning contamination. This one I cannot help as my son likes drinking straight from the Tap ignoring filtered and boiled water. I would advise that you give them water as soon as you notice that they might be thirsty.

I also began to act as vigilante in taking pencils out of his reach. I told the school teachers of the habit, and I advised them to give him an alternative to pencils or supervise him. At home, we resolved to painting with pencils made from plastic, not interesting enough to chew. I thank God for granting me divine WISDOM to deal with the situation.

WAWU episode *HA FINITO! CEST FINI!* This is my simple limited knowledge of French and Spanish meaning IT IS FINISHED. This expression conjures my level of excitement and celebration for the end of pencil chewing episode.

The positive things come out of what life expects to bring nothing but sadness, shame, disgrace, and discomfort but God uses it as a way to enable us find content in ourselves. I started finding strength and comfort within than without. I became more organised and serious about life issues and my relationship with God. I saw God as the answer and my completeness without whom there is nothing but lack. I ensured the kids were in bed at 7 p.m., I will take them to their room, lay them down prayed with them and told them stories. As soon as they fall asleep, I would go to the living room, switch off the electricity bulb, lit my candle and listened to gospel music. In that solemn mood,

I communicated intensely with my inner person and sought spiritual peace, guidance, and grace. I would like to make things clear about this candle. It had no spiritual connotation but I personally enjoyed the serene warmth from a candle.

I went shopping one day and found a lovely indoor plant. I put it in my living room and it looked so beautiful and breath-taking, everyone loved and admired it. Tony, however, decided to help himself with the leaf. I noticed cut leaves on the floor in my living room, and I thought they were possibly getting weak. I then noticed Tony was spitting on the floor and on opening his mouth, I found some green particles. Oh dear!!! This is definitely dangerous. What am I going to do? Another dangerous habit, I wondered, I got really upset, chucked the plant. Well, I guess I don't need to tell you that the habit was over as soon as there was nothing to indulge the leaf-eating. There are situations that need common sense you don't really need a psychologist to clinically observe the situation and give you a solution, all you needed was take action. It is better safe than sorry, it might hurt you getting rid of what you want but you have no alternative. Nothing can equate your child's health it is logical not based on any opportunity cost because there is no choice or forgone alternative.

Most children with autism are not aware of danger and it is your duty as a parent or carer to protect them from these harmful materials. I am lucky with Tony, he is aware of certain dangers and cannot play with them. He would not put his hand inside fire, toaster, or anything dangerous and he would not play with sharp instruments or allow them to be used on him. He even secures the door himself when people leave. Even now that he's grown, he watches me like a hawk when I am helping him shave to ensure he does not get a cut. These episodes of eating inedible substance are called PICA. PICA is characterized by an appetite for substances largely non-nutritive such as ice, clay, chalk, dirt, or sand. According to DSM-IV (Diagnostic statistical Manual of mental disorder) criteria, for these actions to be considered PICA, they must persist for more than one month at an age where eating such objects is considered developmentally inappropriate, not part of culturally sanctioned practice and sufficiently severe to warrant clinical attention(Wikipedia free encyclopedia)

I guess those were early days and most people with autism have PICA. Person diagnosed with autism suffering from PICA should not be given separate diagnosis as a PICA sufferer. PICA has been a major upsetting sensory issue with Tony as he desires to eat dry leaf and toilet roll though it has become more manageable. After several years of taking care of Tony I have come to the conclusion that PICA is related to his moods. It has become like a comforting thing for him. The sensory satisfactions derived from it tend to bring a calming effect for him. This does not excuse the PICA but I give him Magnesium tablet and lots of vegetable like carrots, spinach and cucumber that he can chew on. People who smoke or drink do so when they are under emotional stress so you can imagine our children who are constantly bombarded by unknown elements. Please maintain a diary of your child's behavior and monitor it. Read up on related topics you will always find an answer. Thank God for technology and social media.

CHAPTER 8

Paper Shredder

My son became a paper shredder. When I say shredder, I mean it. He shredded any paper he came across, just like a shredder would do. This was a nightmare because he shredded most of my books. This was such a bad phase; I desperately needed it to end by any means necessary. There was a day his sister was doing her homework and she went to the toilet. By the time she got back, Tony had shredded her homework. She screamed 'mummy' as though someone was hurting her. It was the pain she felt from her brother shredding her work, she felt her brother hated her and was selfish. I had to explain to her that Tony loves her very much and would not do anything to hurt her. I gave her an example of a day I was doing her hair and she was crying, and Tony walked up to me, took the comb, and threw it on the floor because he could not bear to see her in pain. I hugged her and pulled her to sit on my lap. She then asked me 'so what is going to happen to my homework?'

My daughter is so academically conscious, and she loves to do everything perfectly. She currently doing A 'levels in a grammar school and she is doing really well. I told her that I would speak to her teacher to explain what happened and request more time for her to complete the homework.

That was problem solved, but not exactly as Tony's paper shredding phase was still on. The paper shredding was a very difficult phase because Tony had an eagle eye. He picked paper up at a glance and shredded them in seconds. I got tired of this shredding business so I took all papers out of sight as much as I could. I prayed and prayed, hoping for things to change. I thought perhaps it might take much longer for this habit to disappear. Life is so full of ups and downs that sometimes when you think you have got it all figured out, the figure is a figment of your imagination or perhaps rehearsed heartfelt expectations of what you expect to be an outcome of prolonged tearful episodes. I no longer sulk when my expectations are delayed or are not answered. I just release myself to ponder on the positive things life has perfected in my life rather than my shortfalls. The habit stopped on its own when he stopped seeing things to shred. I am blessed with patience, resilience and tolerance which enable me to calm myself in all situations and also to remain positive and expectant.

CHAPTER 9

Teenage Days

My son is now a teenager more or less moving gradually into adulthood. He is quite tall 6.2 and weighs over 70 kg and very well built. He goes to school but not quite, as my life is very unsettled whenever he is at school. There was a period the school was phoning me almost every day at work to complain to me about my son's autistic behaviours. They said he was self-harming which they called EPISODES and sometimes the bus escorts and the driver would say he had a Fit. How can he have Epileptic Fit if he does not suffer from Epilepsy? It would not have been absence seizure, but ignorance, he was self harming and they named it 'Fit'. These drivers and escorts need to be properly trained, or else they will cause more harm than good, though some of them mean well.

It was like a nightmare, nightmare upon nightmare, I was dreading days as I associate days with trouble. It was very unsettling for me at work, though I was blessed and had favour from all my managers. Sometimes I had to leave work to pick up my son as the school would not keep him. It was getting too much my annual leave was finishing too quickly and I was looking very unserious at work. I thought about the predicament and decided to write to the school detailing why they should not be contacting me with such issues as the school is specialised in autism and I am not. If my son is ill then it is my responsibility to take him home until he gets better. I thought he was progressing until in his year nine when the school proved me wrong. I did an assessment of my son's progression only to realise how far he has regressed. It is very painful and the school system for these children is more like a tick box exercise being funded without assessment as to the progression of these children. School for my son, as far as I am concerned, is like a recreational centre with no expectations but a constant strain on tax payers. No one questions the school as everyone comes up with excuses that autism is a wide spectrum and children regress or plateau at certain stages of their life. Perhaps they should tell these stories to the marines because the sailors won't believe the story. These are mere frivolous excuses as autism is the only diagnosis without an expert or cure; no one knows what it is, where it came from, and how to deal with it. The school complained he hits himself so hard and termed it as 'self-harming episodes' which is common with people in autistic spectrum. I could hardly comprehend why a school that claims to work with children in the spectrum should call a parent to take their child home for being autistic, my son was regularly penalised for being autistic and for his physical built. The school is threatened by my little mouse built—what an irony of life. I suppose if they had taken time to know him they would have noticed that he is so angelic, passive, and innocent. His built and height speaks for him, he is already prejudged before contact. School became like a nightmare. Tony became very unsettled and unhappy. I forgot to tell you that Tony is very sensitive and senses when people do not like him much. He also dislikes people who speak impolitely as he is well mannered himself and uses 'please and thank you.

Whenever he recalls school in his ECHOLIAC speeches he mentions some horrid languages people use. I wish most of the time that I can home school my son but for the fact that I needed to earn an income. He has suffered in the hands of ignorant people who claim to have a wealth of knowledge. In the process of all these self-harming episodes he damaged his outer ear. It became shaped more like a curly flower. I took him to the hospital, the doctor inserted needle and there was no pus or blood coming out of the piercing. He was given antibiotics but to no avail. The doctor suggested plastic surgery to which I declined. The boy has suffered enough to be subjected to plastic surgery was unnecessary. The day my friend saw it she cried. You cannot understand how deeply it hurts to see your flesh and blood go through these. Autism is a very nasty disorder and no one should even wish it on their enemy. The lack of support from professionals is very alarming, people see parents with children diagnosed with autism as doing their duty as parents. Autism is one disorder people don't understand. Physical disability, deafness, or blindness is obvious and majority empathise with it. A child with autism is seen as disruptive and uncontrollable, certain public abnormal behaviour is perceived as poor parental upbringing or perhaps lack of boundaries instilled.

We as parents, try as much as possible to alleviate the social effects of autism by working with our children at home and teaching them family values, though our hands are tied with regards to assimilation, as we cannot induce imaginative comprehension. People with autism find it very difficult to understand why certain things are the way they are, and you cannot blame them. They sometimes see words as pictures and colours as words spoken, everyday overview of life and its continuum is a farfetched intellectual exercise which will become problematic if enforced on people with autism. Why border to aggravate them, it would be perfect to know exactly where to draw the line when working with them or else you, as a professional or family, will become ineffective. I have recently come across parents whose children go to respite homes or schools and it is obvious that they are ill treated in that environment. It will be great if parents are given opportunity to carry on the spot checks in such environment. If they can have prison visitors to ensure prisoners are well cared for, what of our children who are void of any criminal activity-who is watching over them? Who is supervising there quality of care? No one, but I will leave you as a parent and carer to think on thChapter 9

Just before the exclusion

Tony woke up this morning having one of the autistic moments. It was a school day and I got him showered and dressed for school. He came downstairs for breakfast; normally I would give him yoghurt to aid the lining of his bowel and improve bowel movement.

Unfortunately, he started bingeing on various foods other

than his normal yoghurt. I knew straight away that this is an alarm bell ringing. I knew he was definitely going to be uncomfortable and cranky at school. When the school bus arrived, I made it clear to the bus escort that Tony might not be in the best of his moods.

What just happened was comfort eating; and we all do that sometimes. A lot of people diagnosed with autism sometimes binge eats - but what is usually seen is the external behavioural struggle enhanced by the internal anxiety that led to that. What is there to alleviate the horrid feeling inside which no one can feel but them? What is inside food I wonder, that tends to act as a kick to revitalise and add vigour to our inner being - just for few minutes? When normal people binge they suffer from stress or perhaps depression, but when people diagnosed with autism binge, it becomes part of the spectrum disorder.

Label! Label!! Label!!! Let us move away from autistic diagnosis and think like normal people. The average non-achiever would contemplate self-harming, suicide, avoid social interaction and communicate less. Our society and generation are not thinking about finding solutions and researching on why these things happen. Life is worrisome and day-to-day challenges of life trigger anxiety. Something has to give in - the feeling or the circumstance. It is a microwave, fast food generation, if we don't understand it, recommend a placebo, and that does it. Pretend the problem is being solved; meanwhile no one really has a clue; autism is a mind-blowing ailment. It has challenged the greatest of scientists and till date, it is still a wonder. The welfare system has made people dependent on it rather than encourage ways to make people get better and move on and out of state-dependency.

Back to the story about what happened at school. The school phoned me around 12pm to come and collect Tony as he was self-harming. Thank God, I was self-employed at the time - it made me more flexible. I called a cab to take me to school to pick him up; meanwhile his carer had come as pre-planned to take care of him whilst I attended a meeting.

We both decided to go to Tony's school to pick him up. On getting to the school, the class teacher was looking all flustered. The teaching assistant, who looked more composed, went to get Tony from somewhere. She said to me in a very unfriendly, aggressive tone (without concern as to Tony's welfare, more like, thank God you're here we can now; get rid of him!).

She told me, 'Next time he has PICA we are going to call 999' (more like we are going to section him!). I ignored her comment, since I perceived it was coming from ignorance and frustration. How could you nonchalantly threaten a parent with sectioning her child? Tony's carer asked her, 'what do you mean by PICA?", which she reluctantly explained to him. He was confused as to how any form of PICA could warrant sectioning. At that moment I decided to just play DUMB because that is how I perceived the whole scenario to be. When we took Tony home, the carer was with him whilst I went for my engagement.

On getting to the place, the first phone call came from Social Services who needed to know if I was fine, as the class teacher had phoned them to say that I and my daughter were in danger at home as Tony would attack us.

I was confused and I asked the Social Services person if, in my 18 years of raising this child, I had ever called them for assistance or could not cope or had ever been in danger?

She apologised and said she thought I needed help. What cheek? I just could not fathom why the class teacher did that; it looked very malicious and vindictive. For crying out loud, he is not in a mainstream school. How could she have taken laws into her hands to speak or lie on behalf of a mother? Not only did she want to section him, she wanted him to end up in a care home, not in a college environment. And we wonder why the system is having funding problems, when people in certain position use tax payer's money ignorantly. Why should children be in care in the first place when there are relatives willing to care for them? The excuse is that they are dysfunctional themselves.....really, or the professional in question has personal vendetta.

At this moment I just needed to cry; if I was wealthy enough to pay for a private school and not dependent on the state paying for his fees, he would not be in this situation, would he? If Tony did not have special needs, she would not have a clue that Tony existed. It was a very bad experience and it left me suspicious of professionals working with Tony till date. My dear, my day had not finished yet, but had just begun with stress from professionals. My phone rang again, this time it was from CAMHS. The lady claimed the class teacher sent a referral letter to them. This time the caller was a psychiatrist. I asked her why the referral was sent to a psychiatrist, that my son is diagnosed with Autism and more so the teacher had no right to refer my son without my consent, and I am meant to see the content also.

She apologised, and said she would send it to the Department that specialises in Autism and also send me a copy of the referral form they were sent. Hmmm, a few days later this referral arrived. Not surprisingly, it contained untrue accounts of events: that Tony had come home with a black eye. I was dumbfounded, my daughter was flabbergasted and the carer was shocked! None of us could believe it; it was frightening that a professional person could conjure such lies against an innocent child. That did it for me!!!!!!!!!! I lost respect for the school authority. My son has never come home with a black eye; I guess they needed to say that to make their referral look urgent.

Please I beg you reader, do not allow professionals to cajole you into accepting non-existent issues in pretence of either getting funding for your child or patronising you. It is a pity that most people referred to agencies are not meant to be referred, and it impacts greatly on tax payers and has a huge financial impact.

It is an overwhelming experience to care for a child diagnosed with Autism and more so the compounded mistrust from professionals who work with them. My dear, Autism is a very draining ailment to the victim, the carer and the observer. You are on high alert all year round and the only thing that calms you is when you decide to switch off from eventualities that flaunt themselves unexpectedly. Autism is callous and fearless; it keeps you unguarded and vulnerable. I expect professionals working with these children to have passion, compassion, commitment and care as one of the attributes they need. Unfortunately, people take on jobs to earn money and improve their status; our children are left with people who just don't care. Perhaps I am speaking on behalf of most parents who are too busy with life assignments to focus on changing and challenging the inevitable. In my vocabulary, there is nothing that cannot be changed, human beings are creatures of comfort zones and they don't particular want to relocate. Freda is packed and ready to move on to the next zone provided it will make a possible, positive change.

A mother's Cry - AUTISM

Have I not shed enough tears?

Have I not wondered enough in dismay?

Swallowing every tear

That dripped constantly from my eyes

And every watery fluid from my nose

Yet you want to cut my expectations short

And thwart my destiny

Have I not been bruised enough?

Yet you add salt to worsen the pain

Why do you hurt me and soothe the pain

Perhaps you are twisted and disgruntled

I am no longer afraid but you wish I was

So that you can import nightmare

I am no longer sad and confused

But you want to regularly give me detailed

Negative experiences to jump start my sadness

I tried to be bold and strong

But you walked into my life fully geared

With machinery to destabilise me

You are a terror, I know that!

So why terrorise me

We have never encountered each other

In the past and present life

Why are you in my life?

And in my innocent child's progress

You are a master of regression

Diverting your chaos to children

You are a coward

You hide under the umbrella of children

Shielded by diagnosis and tagging

You are a chameleon

And that is why every victim is different

They call you an ailment without prognosis

I call you a demon

Without a body

Looking for various vulnerable bodies to possess

I no longer ponder on who and what you are up to

But on how to exorcise you

You might think you are playing games

But time will come for me to say CHECK MATE

Game over!!!!

And that time is now.

Further contact with the school

I would like to say emphatically that the reasons why I mentioned Tony's experiences within the academic wall is the fact that, it is part of what formed and deformed him, what made and unmade him, what moulded him and unmolded him. You can never disconnect the two. He had his heights and his lows. Like I said earlier he had his moments of progression and his recent regression all down to the school. The school though did not accommodate my child but where able to meet some children's need. They say one man's meat is another man's poison and one man's mansion is another man's hut, your angel can be my demon and your saviour my destroyer, It is important that you build relationship first with people to know if they can accommodate you and also if it is suitable for you and your needs. Life is unpredictable so are people, sometimes it could be fate that opens door of opposition to certain people and to others doors of proposition. No matter what doors is open to you and your family I suggest you work in, fully geared with assertiveness and open mindedness. I would suggest do not base your conclusion on what others have seen and experienced be bold and curious, try it out, but do not allow yourself to be mesmerised by bureaucratic jargon. There were misunderstandings and misgivings but what is important is that till date all professionals are working towards the same goal and that is, ensuring that Tony's welfare and needs are paramount in the whole matter and measures to meet them are being put in place. I would at this point give kudos to the social services for their effort in ensuring that things worked out well between my family and the school. And also to the head teacher for listening to the outcry of a mother by ensuring my grievances where looked into. Tony has been at home so to speak till date since December with support from social services and the school. I salute all the employers of the school who have been working with my son, they are not high ranking school personnel but they showed passion and enthusiasm in ensuring that my son is supported at home. It has not been easy having strangers walk in and out of your home, my home is my sacred space, but oh well, sometimes we need to bend over to accommodate eventualities that life casually throws on our way. My son is happy and self- harming episodes decreased. I am at peace that I have time to work with my son preparing him for another school environment. ….Finger crossed.

CHAPTER 10

Tony's Exclusion from School

Sometimes you wonder if it just pours and drenches rather than rains and just gets you wet. Life journey can be painful and kicks you where you never expect it to. Some have it all beautiful and rosy and others have it like thorns. Some cry regularly others are always in a laughter mood. You are dependent on people you are more or less forced to coexist. Like the old saying 'no man is an island' you can never be self-sufficient, we depend on each other one way or the other which is a painful reality. Sometimes I wish I was an island with all the amenities and facilities to exist without depending on others. When you get to my level which I pray you don't, you will begin to want to void yourself of other people's company as you realise the constant disappointment from people. My son was expelled from an autistic school; they claim he was self-harming by hitting himself and they needed to safeguard him against himself. I personally needed to ascertain few things from the school—children with autism are bound to hit themselves as most of them have a high threshold for pain. What he did, was it uncommon in diagnosis of autism?

Did you see any evidence of physical injury as harming oneself can only be evidenced through bruises, cuts, and swelling? None of the above questions were answered and the conclusion is that he was expelled without any reason. I was made to spend time at home with my son, not that those times are not invaluable but the fact that he was deprived of extra curriculum due to his physical attributes. It is late now; maybe I should have customised him and asked God to give me a small child that will pose no threat to anyone. I am still looking for a school that will engage him adequately and pray that God will enable me to succeed. It is difficult for you to stand to defend a child who cannot give an account of incidents. How will you start and what exactly can you say. No matter how eloquent and a great orator you may be or well-articulated your defence may be, it will not make any difference as the defendant stands mute. Even in the court of law or interrogation process, you have the right to silence and that does not make you guilty. I guess that is the court process, but in day to day dealings muteness signifies weakness and throwing in the towel. If I throw in the towel who is going to fight for my son? I know the situation is not a battle ground but I am being fired and bombarded without any thought as to my state of mind. No one cares to know what is happening to me and how I handle my life on a daily basis, the social service call our children 'children in need' but has anyone knocked on my door since he was diagnosed with autism to ask what his needs are and how am I coping? The society does not intervene earlier until the situation is bad. I wonder how many families are stuck in a state of helplessness awaiting the professionals to say hello. Children with autism are wonderful and loving children but the ailment can be very consuming to carers as your life is moulded into an autistic pattern in order to remould your child into your own world.

The 999 Call

What will you tell the police or ambulance when they come around to arrest a person diagnosed with autism? My dear, this question is my dilemma—I cannot comprehend my son being threatened with 999 calls because the school said he was self-harming; I was very confused as to why. He was not physically attacking anyone or being violent but being autistic. Firstly, if he did not have any problem he would have been going to a mainstream school. How many doctors discharge their patients because they are presenting with symptoms of the ailment. How many psychiatric patients are discharged from hospital due to the fact that they are having psychotic episodes, I believe special schools should be equipped to handle symptoms within the spectrum. We are living in a very cruel world where things are not exactly as they seem. People say one thing and do another; if your face and physic fits you will be accommodated without prejudice. Who inspects what happens in special needs school.....no one, they claim Ofsted, really? Do they have a clue what traumatic experiences these children go through? It is very simple and self explanatory for a difficult child to be locked up in isolation until it is time to go home. Poor parents the drama never gets unfolded we all seem to be blindfolded into accepting they are doing us a huge favour. In my case it would be easier for the school if my son had been dosed with psychotic medications to enable him become a Zombie all day. Then he will be kept in isolation whilst the teachers have a field day. On second thought, perhaps they were contemplating on sectioning my child. The act of sectioning was introduced in 1983—this is a part of mental health act to gain legal permission to detain someone for treatment against their will. This is the bit I worry as ignorant people out there, cannot differentiate between mental illness and autism. Some people even criminalise autism. Where exactly do we draw the line, does autistic people have the necessary *mens rea* or criminal responsibility to have intent to commit crime. Many high functioning people diagnosed with autism have been found to access security code and hack computer systems. At what point will the public draw the line when it comes to people diagnosed with autism. They might have attacked people but without intention. Does it mean a lesser degree of punishment or none? Is the court going to accept diminished responsibility for plea bargaining or shall the court completely dismiss the allegation. People use provocation or contributory negligence as reason for getting a lesser sentence. Autism is like a remote control that controls settings in the children's life. You need to be acquainted with the remote control before you can change the battery. I guess there are so many inmates in prison occupying those hideous prison cell diagnosed with autism or perhaps not diagnosed at all, it is very easy to diagnose a lesser functioning person with autism as the high functioning ones are very difficult to diagnose. Whether high or low functioning what is important is that every parent should have a voice and advocate for their children to ensure fair treatment of all and diversification of opinions, strategy, and policies. You cannot accept every professional opinion as being the truth. Read, research, respond, and recognise the symptoms your child is presenting with similar diagnosis. A mother never gets it wrong. Let us all come together and join hands to protect our children from an impending bureaucratic crisis that will endanger their wellbeing. Never accept any diagnosis on face value research, read and then respond.

TAC meeting for Tony

The full meaning of the TAC meeting is Team around the Child, It can be defined as an evolving team of practitioners who have contact with the child or young person and family on a regular basis and who provide practical support and advice with and to those who are able to work directly with the child or young person and family as appropriate. (http://www.sandwell.gov.uk/info/200219/children/677/common_assessment_framework/6). Please I would advise you that if you have a weak constitution you need to take care of that before reading this chapter as it embodies on toilet allegations made by Mr X from his school who has never met my child. I was invited to TAC meeting after my child was excluded from the school, permit me to be ignorant. I am just wondering if the TAC should have been held prior to his exclusion and if the essence of the TAC Is as follows; to identify the needs of the child, to discuss with professionals the actions the family will take in order to assist the child and looking at the child and the family's level of need. This meeting didn't. It seemed as if the meeting was geared towards positively trying to identify his needs but it didn't but managed to serve as an avenue to justify my son's exclusion. Mr X to my dismay started recapping events that took place even as far back as over 4 years ago but one thing that devastated me and made me ill with headache for more than a week was the highlight of the day -the poo consumption. As the drama unfolded, the scenes enacted by Mr X left me in a state of shock and disappointment. As I have always had so much respect for professionals. At that meeting he mentioned that my son was excluded due to safe guarding issues, as my son was feeding on his faeces in the toilet. I must say I was horrified at the professional's lack of tactics and diplomacy. I know we being British are very good and respected all over the world for Diplomacy we don't just vomit our guts out carelessly but he did. It was like a lion waiting to devour the prey or a hunter that missed the trap and got himself entrapped. He spoke with so much hatred and guilt, just like a defendant brought before the witness stand. I was angry, but at the same time I felt embarrassed for him. Trust me! My Masters degree in Crime and Litigation was not in vain, I started cross examining him. Firstly, I needed to know why I was not told this when I attended my son's review meeting 2 weeks before his exclusion. If, that is the case it then means my son has not been safeguarded in the school environment. He gave a GCSE chemistry lecture in all manner of toxic substances found in faeces and how he could possibly spit the content on someone and cause them blindness or HIV, what a jerk! I guess my whole family is blind from poo toxins. (Laugh out loud). Why I was not told, I just don't understand? Why was the incident not recorded with the school nurse? It was as if a bombshell was dropped. At that point he became confused.com (laugh out loud). I emphatically told him that he was lying not wavering in any form. This is my child's life and I am not going to allow people to gamble or toy with it, I am his voice and advocate. My shock is not just from what he said but the fact that our vulnerable children are in the hands of strange people. Fate has a way of spurring us to move away from impending plot, that explains the divine orchestrated exclusion or my son would have been sectioned by the school.

I inhaled a breath of satisfaction that my son is no longer a tool in the hands of the sculptor otherwise he would have melted away perhaps in a mental health ward. My friend was with me at the meeting, and Mr X owed me a duty of care and professional responsibility in terms of data protection. Supposedly, he was meant to clarify or ask for my permission if I needed such information to be disclosed in front of my friend, even though it was a lie. Sometimes I wonder what kind of professionals are in sensitive positions, perhaps it is about time tax payers reconsider people they spend huge salaries on. These people are like walking hazards waiting to detonate in ignorant families. I left the room because I was feeling very dizzy and unwell as a result of what just transpired. The social worker and my friend came out with me to check if I was okay. When I went back to the room he apologised, he thought he was attending a different meeting. Interestingly, it was carefully dismissed and dusted nicely under the carpet. If you are a parent reading this, please I would advise you to ensure you prepare for every meeting, do not entrust your situation with any professional. I felt alone at the meeting apart from an inner strength and my friend who accompanied me. All the professionals believed him, it was as if I was dramatising or living in self- denial.

My state of mind is far from their assumption, I would accommodate help if the help was positive and the concern existed. This incident is a shock to my system so to speak. I will pause to thank God that what the enemy meant for bad he resurrected it to my excellence and fame. Dear friends, the issue the school initially highlighted before the TAC meeting was that they could not safeguard Tony against himself. I argued that bit, because I believe that, self-harming is not a justifiable reason to exclude a child with Autism. Self -harming in children diagnosed with Autism are not separate diagnosis with Autism are they? I am sure by now you will be able to answer this question; I will leave you to it. What I gathered from all these meetings is that my son is left to hit his head as long as it lasts provided the school and staff are not in any commotion. I do not allow self-harming at home because there is likelihood that it might injure him internally. He is a big lad, so you can imagine the impact on his person. They should have sought professional input regarding self-harming rather than conjure non - existence concern that has no bearing with anything. My son hardly self- harms frequently at home as they said he does at school. I take out time to work with him at home to alleviate such incidents. I have studied him and I know that the self-harming has causation. The school said that it is unpredictable, but I say it is predictable if you care to understand Tony. It could come as a result of recap of memory of bad previous incidence, boredom, social phobia, attention seeking, ill health, too much noise, body temperature, hunger, tiredness, fits, too much food, dairy products, inability to sleep or insomnia and mostly sensory needs. Even though some of us are not diagnosed with Autism we have an element of social anxiety phobia and that is what these children go through and much more. It is important that you as a parent take out time and identify the causation and minimise it, otherwise your child will be injured. We are living in a busy world but saving your child's life will go a long way in reducing the care you will give them when they get hurt. I am always with him when I am at home unless he is sleeping. The role is not exactly very simple and neither is it a rocket science but mother's instinct and love makes it work. Please develop a positive relationship with your child and study his moods as he studies yours, my son is good at it and knows when I am happy, sad or worried. Don't throw in the towel yet until you have had a shower (which means don't give up yet).

We later reconvened another day to have a review meeting. All the professionals gathered round the table with my invisible self in the midst of it all. The chapter opened to unveil the school agenda and that is to ensure that no school accepted my son. The review was strongly worded like prosecutor's case statement with lots of bad character evidence against my son the defendant, poor boy! If only I could downsize him perhaps all will be at peace. The review document still contained the same toilet hearsay evidence despite my opposition letters To Whom It May Concern, it didn't make any difference. I refused to sit amongst professionals going through falsified documentation of my son's review. I needed to know where, when and who saw this incident. I asked if pictures was taken in the toilet and was given the usual officious reply, we are not allowed to use camera in the toilet', yes that I know, but any recorded evidence of this matters? They said no, they finally decided to cross it out from his report, as there was no evidence. Friends! Please weep for me if you can, I thought this can only happen in the 3rd world countries where I originally come from. Some people want to keep their job no matter what it takes. Some people want to protect their interest no matter who is hurt in the process. In these, where do we draw a huge line, this child is disabled for crying out loud. It is a shame! It is important for you to understand that none of these people knew my child personally or made an effort to study him even for a second; I guess that's too demanding.

Encounter with the Educational Psychologist

I would frankly tell you that she was sitting on edge when I met her, but I was afraid for her in case she slips. When she opened her mouth I could perceive a lack of concern and aggression, her input was just like a tick box exercise manipulated by the school authority. She said to me patronisingly, 'I hope you are prepared as some of the issues the school highlighted might be upsetting'. I said not to worry, I have read and seen it in the previous review, as lies have no boundaries, does it? I asked her, pardon me, have you met Tony before or observed the young man whom you have tabled a lot of clinical evidence and findings. She said no, great!

Where do I start with this one, as the whole report was not a true observation of the subject but recounted hearsay evidence? I asked how she can rely on the class teacher's evidence than clinically observe Tony. She said she can base her judgement on what the class teacher said, there is nothing wrong with that. I rest my case. The more I meet these professionals the more confused I get as If I am the only sane person, is it just me? Sometimes I wish they can walk a second in my shoe and see what becomes of them. This is not just about promotions and salary but about passion, compassion, commitment and genuine care. I am carrying a placard for 'US' parents with special children and I pray the world will halt to attend to our cry. As if taking care of our children is not enough work, they want to cripple us too, if we get handicapped what will happen to our children. Should the society not be empowering us to just thrive but excel. It seems as if we are living in a labelling society where dependency is encouraged. What kind of profit or gain emanates from labelling children? I guess if these labels were visible 80% of children will have an invisible forehead.

CHAPTER 11

Tony's Sister

Tony is my brother and I love him to bits, though I miss normal teases and banter which you expect from a teenage brother. It is difficult for me because I wish he can drive me around to the mall and perhaps watch my friends develop a crush on him.

Also I wish I can show him off as my body guard and watch him warn boys not to come near me. I wish he could fight my corner sometimes, because he has so much physical attributes—he is tall, big, and handsome. I learnt a lot from having him as a brother. I grew up quickly helping mum to keep an eye on him. It seems nice playing big sister but mum always reminds me consciously that Tony is my big brother and I should respect him. I watch him cry sometimes and I feel sad and wish I can make things better. In my younger days I used to be jealous of Tony as the world revolves around him. Mum seems to pay so much attention even to his breath. People seem fascinated by him. I became more like a normal annoying little girl while everyone lavishes him with attention. Even when he is naughty it seem all normal, I just could not comprehend why adults are so blinded by AUTISM. Sometimes I wonder what that thing is—it became more like a spectacular tag rather than anything negative. I watch Mum with so much vigour and vitality trying to make him function normally, I thought by now Mum would have had a PhD in Autism, she read books and attended all kinds of seminars. I did not miss out in my academics, Mum invested money in private tuition to enable me go to a grammar school, which I did. I remember the day his speech came back—we all celebrated—Mum was overjoyed. I watched him do some strange things, particularly removing his milk teeth when they start becoming wobbly. Most of my friends and family say he is really handsome but I don't think they can have a crush on him because of his situation. People love perfect people and no one wants a liability, but when you get to know this liability you are bound to understand their ability to make a woman ceaselessly happy.

Listen, you are every woman's dream—you are kind, sweet, gentle, and loving you will make a fantastic husband in the future.

Above all, you are just like a child with no ability to think or do evil. We all at home have grown up quickly mentally and spiritually as you have equipped us to understand the power of loving even when you don't get a response. The ability to be patience filled with expectations of great and wonders things that we envisage that will manifest in your life. You are going to be 18 years old but we all believe that things will turn around one day and you will live a normal life. I am going to be 16 and I have watched Mum pray for your complete healing since I was born and we are still hopeful. I must say you are lucky to have Mum as your mother; she is a super woman and loves us uncompromisingly. Mum always says if I come back again, I would be like the same child over and over again.

Living with Autism

I have lived and known Autism for the past 18 years and can tell you all about it from my perspective and you can tell me yours. Frankly speaking our experiences can never ever be the same. I can live with my brother without any qualms but you might not withstand him for 5 minutes. We still have sibling rivalry and fighting for our mother's attention and affection. When I was younger I use to be jealous of our mother's relationship with Tony because I have this perception that Tony was her favourite as she spends a lot of time with him and does most personal cares for him. In my opinion I feel he is capable of doing most of them. I guess he takes advantage of mum's vulnerability to play on her intelligence. Our interpretations of our experiences tend to differ as the individual sufferers are unique in their reaction to the ailment. This could be hampered by underlying illness, psychological reaction, emotional anxiety, family dynamics as children who live in dysfunctional family tend to exhibit more ADHD like symptom in conjunction with Autism. Also fear of other people's reaction can make families have more negative reaction and hinder progress in the sufferer. These children are overly sensitive and react even to your heart beat if you care to know. We all have to strive to curtail excessiveness of life like violence, strife, anger and selfishness in order to accommodate these sufferers. The ailment is bad but having an added disadvantage from upbringing makes it a nightmare. Fix up and get your act together if you love your sibling or your child. The adult lascivious and wanton nature of existence have so much impacted on the way young people perceive and deal with situations. An adult must be conscious of the consequences of their behaviour on people that see them as role models. We know children with Autism are clever they pick up words no matter how good or bad. They copy behaviours out of ignorance. All these we know, why don't we try as much as possible to shelter them from public mockery. In my home our mum is very conscious of Tony's external stimuli than any other thing. This emanates from what we eat it has to be organic, free range and less sugar to curb Tony's anxiety and hyperactivity. What is on TV has to be censored to avoid Tony mimicking anything negative on TV. The volume has to be adjusted and the light deemed and we use blackout curtains. Our home is adjusted to fit Tony most times, but it is perfect for me. We hardly have visitors at home as mum hardly visits anyone except if it is very important, mum is like a hermit and a content one indeed. Mum likes herbal stuff and shares them with Tony as for me, I give it a miss I love my sweet stuff. My house is so quiet that you can even hear a pin drop except for my loud music in the bathroom and in my room which mum frowns at most times. As am writing this mum has a jug of hot lemon and lime for her and Tony, I don't envy them, they taste disgusting. Some evenings mum would make a jug of green tea for both of them and I watch them drink with so much interest and curiosity which I keep to myself. Reader, you have work in your hands and a life to make better, please do all you can to ensure you deter them from ruins of external influence and shelter them as much as you can. I am worried sometimes as to how my brother will cope as an adult, the world is cruel and does not give a thus as to how anyone feels or what is going on with them. People are attacked, robbed and humiliated regardless of their ability. Sometimes I wonder if there is hell, because life is hell at present, can it get worse than it is. Pardon me to question the integrity in the present state of man who occupy and walk the earth, virtually everything is inordinate. How come we are shocked that the society is breeding more adults, young people and children on the Autistic spectrum who desire to elope to another vicinity' Autistic world'.

Social life

Tony has no social life but I have, mum, not sure as she hardly goes anywhere but better than Tony. They go for a long drive on Sundays and Tony's carer sometimes comes around too. Mum and Tony are like peas in a pod, they watch TV together and do most things together except when Tony falls asleep and goes to his room. Mum's whole being is glued to Tony's reaction to external stimuli. It is so bad that she can hear Tony cry even when he is miles away, sometimes she runs into his room with so much care and worries, and meanwhile he is snoring. I might feel sorry for him due to his lack of social life, but I do ask myself what is social life and of what benefit are friends who are nowhere to be found when life situation becomes unbearable.

Maturity

We are both getting older and more sensible in certain ways but my brother due to the limitation imposed by Autism has climaxed more in his physiological maturity than the cognitive but that that does not mean that he has not improved tremendously. When I see men of his age I feel really moved by my brother's Autism as it has prevented him from having any aspirations and social life. He is tagged amongst children under 6 years. That is regressing 12 years though he can do quite a lot than them. Life knows how to diminish our expectations and slaughter our desires. Sometime in the future he might like someone or a lady might decide to propose to him. How can we determine the genuineness in their proposal we can only hope and pray. I too will be getting married in the future and pray my husband will see him as a brother too. I just cannot imagine him not doing that, as my brother is and has always been a part of my existence which cannot be thwarted. Mum will be getting older and the demand on me to take most roles is indelible. Some have come on earth for jollification and for others it is about survival. That is why people like us mature mentally and emotionally more than most.

Who would not be blessed to care for a brother who has a big heart and a permanent joy?

My brother is an angel though his wings are clamped disabling his ability to do exploits and guard all his beloved. Yet he manages to do all he can in his limited life resources. When I was younger if he sees me crying in my room he will go to mum and take her to me. Though he does not say much but his action generates goodness

The School Disco

I went to a grammar school and usually we have disco every quarter with the neighbouring boys' grammar school. Even though am in a place of enjoyment I still think of my brother as I have a close connection with him. When I see boys his age I wish my brother did not have disability and can function normally like them. Whenever I come across young boys with mild autism who are being bullied by their peer it breaks my heart because young people can be very callous and reckless, and will sometimes go out of their way to be mean to each other. These kids are susceptible to being bullied by their peer due to their communication and social impairment. I was standing with friends from my school when I noticed this young unassuming boy being pushed to the wall by other boys. They kept pulling and taunting him yet he kept quiet and did not even say a word or react in any way. Some others joined laughing and calling him names. I did not like what was going on, I pulled one of them aside to ascertain what was going on, they said the boy is Autistic, Just that? When has nature's handicap become a criminalised impairment? Is it a crime to be different? I kept bombarding myself with these questions but no answers. I stepped forward and demanded they stop immediately. After all these I was taken aback as to where I got the boldness and impetus from to stand for what is right, made me proud of myself and amazed me. Youth is another word for excitement and selfishness. I guess as am writing this am speaking to siblings of young people diagnosed with Autism. You need to keep the fate and rise up above the limitations of life, assist and support your sibling not to be bullied or terrorised by more able peers. There is a common Ibo saying that' when you wear rags you get addressed as a beggar. When you cloth yourself in affluence you get prostration. The world is class and realistic conscious, too busy with technology and self-worship than to acknowledge the imperfections thrown at other people's lives. Young people should be educated from the beginning to learn how to cope with the most demining situations as they can come, unannounced one way or the other no matter how mild. The amount of suicide happening amongst young people is on the increase due to dysfunctional homes and poor parenting. Do not resolve to laxity because life issues have not paid you a visit yet, but be alert and lay ambush because it is an impulsive intruder with no remorse or empathy. I am compelled to say to you that I am unmoved and unshaken by Autism the more it rages the more I am equipped. The school disco was lovely with lights and music, it was exciting but I was long gone mentally and spiritually flooded with anxiety as to what the future will hold for my brother. The whole stage was set and the casts dramatized in such equivocal manner, everything seemed random nothing was in sequence. It was as if I was the only actor following the script of life as written. In that strange solemn moment, I noticed tears gliding through my friend's eyes, for one second I thought I was alone in this stage of life, glad someone could empathise. The rest were dancing and playing, having fun, as for me the dance was over in my little world just waiting for the music to stop and the disco light to fade. I was grimaced by the sudden patronising behaviour of one of the students who joined the tearful crew, knowing full well they were oblivious of what transpired. My thought was, is this mockery or playing stupid. We young people love joining the crowd without knowing what happened and how it all started.

A day with Tony

Good Morning

Yes, it is morning woken up with so much expectation for the rest of the day. As soon as my eyes pops open my heart begins to beat fast as to what to expect from my brother. I just wondered if he will be waking up with wailings or a quiet morning. I am always weary as to what the mornings will bring or perhaps he will walk into my room while my eyes are hardly open and then shout 'TV' or just ignore me completely and walk down stairs or to mum's room. When he starts crying in the morning it completely throws my routine off balance. If mum is away on a meeting, then am in for it. He will wake me up to change the channel so many times. If he ignores me, then am in for a deep cleaning venture as Tony would empty the fridge content on the dining table. Toast and butter all the bread in the fridge and perhaps not even have a bite. Then concentrate on the juice and empty all the content. 'Tough luck' if we have cereal, Tony would pour most of the content in a bowl then help himself to only a hand full. Sometimes I will manage to get myself downstairs only to see the scare, a messed up kitchen. Mum usually keeps his breakfast on the table before going out, but that is not adequate for my brother, he must make a mess. I feel guilty as mum always keeps the house spick and span. I tend to apologise a lot for my brother's mess, but mum always says to me, please don't, it is not your fault. It is interesting to note that mum always cleans the house before going to sleep. I guess in case she wakes up late. Mum is quite an interesting person, she always prepares for eventualities of the day, like a knock on the door first thing in the morning. Who knows?

Afternoon

We are both at school oblivious of what the other person is up to, but to reconvene at home later. My brother can be a handful; notwithstanding, I still miss him and look forward to seeing him.

Sometimes I would buy him snacks on my way back from school. I always wondered how his been all day and pray he has a good day. We as a family are very conscious of Tony's previous experiences in his former school and we think of it from time to time and pray it will never reoccur in his present. We have been tutored by an ailment to be too careful and anxious. If it is weekend, then the unfortunate person to sit in the leaving room will be forced to change channel for Tony every 20 minutes and clean the carpet from crumbs that must have fallen from Tony's snack. We try as much as possible to ensure he eats in the kitchen sometimes mum who set the rules tend to break it herself, particularly when she is tired. My house is usually quiet all the time accept when my neighbour's children come to play with my mum, kids love coming to my house to spend time with mum, not sure why they like her so much. Well she is very kind and loving, more so patient and tolerant. She also spends time jumping rope and trampoline with them, that is why sometimes I say to her, you are so immature, but not in a disrespectful manner.

Night time

We have all said good night to each other hoping that Tony will sleep. Mum will visit our rooms sometimes to anoint and pray for us. His sleeping pattern varies; he sleeps before 12am sometimes but most times especially weekends he goes to bed after 2am. He might even be awake till 5am, and mum keeps awake with him. They both watch telly and mum falls asleep on the couch until Tony taps mum to say 'bed time. Off he goes to bed praying that he will sleep all through. I feel sorry for mum her role though unpaid but she carries it out with so much diligence, 24 hours a day of mum's time, more than 17hours on weekends is spent by mum caring for Tony. I just don't know how mum finds time to do masters in law without failing any course work, write her books and work yet take care of my brother and yet manage to keep the house spotless.

She even does all the laundry in the house and cleans all the rooms in the house. She is indeed superwoman, these I noticed when she ran the local government election, she did say she had trillions of angels assisting her, I can see that for sure because the way her fliers were distributed in 2 days was amazing. Mother's instinct must be rather strong, I don't know how mum hears Tony crying in her sleep and wakes up just 10 minutes before he starts crying.

Autism is a costly ailment it drains, it empties and leaves the family penniless but fulfilled, in the sense that the victim is still in the care and comfort of their home with beloved and significant others. Most times I feel sorry for our mum as she keeps replacing stuff at home. My brother cannot sleep on a bed as he keeps damaging most of the beds in his room. Am sure you are wondering what I mean by damage, he rocks back and forth when he is anxious about something or perhaps upset. He is a big lad and when he rocks it impacts a great deal on that furniture. We had a beautiful red antique sofa which lasted less than 3 years. My brother has not always been like this, but it suddenly came on, unaware. We are not sure if it is hormonal or age attributed, or linked to advancement in Autism or his school. I was worried about this head banging until I paid a visit to (Dr Greene. com) and several other paediatricians who dealt with signs of Autism in children. It is believed that body and head banging are normal in child development due to when the child is growing up mum uses rocking therapy as a way to either rock the child to sleep or soothe any pain or discomfort. This habit normally stops when the child is 4 years' old, needs to be evaluated if it goes further. This is very stimulating for children and helps them sleep or settle. It is more common in boys than girls. The good news is that toddlers and infants cannot get brain damage from the act; rather it shows a sign of intelligence in children, they say.

The best way to stop a habit is not to acknowledge it; they are usually a sign of attention and tantrum. Some children with Autism head bang as a result of over active external sensory stimuli. It could be due to a sound, smell, light, pain and fear. These are difficult to denote from a person with Autism who cannot explain how they feel from time to time. Rocking is a fulfilling therapy for people with Autism and due to his age it becomes very problematic and socially awkward and unacceptable behaviour. Some Professionals will advise you not to stop this rhythm in people with Autism, as it is inhumane. They say it is therapeutic and stopping it is like diverting them to a more serious alternative. You just cannot enforce digression without dealing with the causation. It is invaluable to discover why the child gets themselves into that awful pitiful state. Mother and child attachment during nurturing is very important. Normal children and young people over the period of growth and development discover a soothing technique a teddy bear, soft toys, and other methods including a blanket. Remember children suck their thumb, suck their tongue and lips as a comforting technique and when it comes to head banging people are quick to diagnose their children with Autism. Do not live in fear my friend, or jump quickly into labelling mode, but investigate and assist, if you cannot, then consult experts, but never assist them with the diagnosis. We are living in high tech world hence the huge number of self – diagnosis, as most people Goggle and diagnose them before medical practitioner does. They invoke the symptoms and psychologically it manifests. Perhaps doctors should recommend PLACEBO for the hypochondriac amongst us, who enjoy attention. Head banging could be tantrum, anger or anxiety, whatever it is we at home are taking it one day at a time, optimistic that we shall find solutions. If you have one, we don't mind. He moved to our black solid leather Sofa, most of the back rest are all damaged. Thank God for mum she just smiles and says' All is well'. Really!!!!!!!!!!!!!

It is embarrassing and uncomfortable to have damaged chairs in your lounge, don't forget am a teenager and seeks to impress. Sometime we went on holidays and my brother broke the bed from rocking, mum was told to pay for the broken bed, poor mummy!!! And we had to fly back to London few days earlier to avoid further unpredictable damages.

But mum tries as much as possible to make things look good and creative. The money mum would have lavished on me is spent on endless replacement and I wish we could spend it on alternative. Don't get me wrong I am not selfish but just being a teenager, self -centred and innovative. Sometimes I wish I can step out of my comfort zone and digress a little bit to an unusual setting where the abnormally of life have not transpired. It takes me, and me alone to handle the pressure imposed by Autism and still look nice.

Please don't call me vain. If you have been to where I have been and where am coming from perhaps you will be seeking a solemn moment where life impediment is locked up.

At the moment I am writing this, my WIFI at home and BT line has been damaged, as my brother rocks back and forth it impacts on not just the chair also the wall behind it. The wall is fully destroyed and the socket box behind destroyed. He could injure himself thank God the walls are not strong. We all are forced to use our mobile internet judiciously to avoid too much mobile phone bill. This month I am predicting it will take a huge toll on all of us, but I pray for divine intervention. You can imagine how much the phone bill came up to hmmm…..500 pounds and the Wi-Fi repair 100 pounds. I am sure you are wondering how I ran up 500 pounds bill, well on holidays in Spain. I needed to entertain myself as the whole holiday premise revolves around my brother's moods. Most times, I just leave him and mum to get on with it, watching cartoon and boring programme. As for me, I needed my music and a movie, so I used the Wi-Fi on my phone….'silly Billy'. It should have occurred to me that I was running a huge bill. At that point I was too bewildered or disorientated by my brother's autistic behaviour than being reasonable, well a reasonable person my age would not succumb to the temptation of such an expensive leisure. You fail to consider the emotional and psychological state of the person in question.

This time, we both need a spank but for the upgrade of our status 'Teenager and 'Adult', poor mum. She knows how to deal with stressful situations like these, she just pretends they are never there, completely switched OFF. Guess what! She refused to pay the bill oblivious of my facial expressions and moody looks. The Wi-Fi got repaired first, that means I can have Wi-Fi regardless of the phone bill being settled. Mum decided not to pay the bill at once in order to teach me a lesson about being extravagant, nonchalant and careless. I must say it takes a strong disciplined person to raise teenagers and still be in control. Parents easily lose control when they lack consistency. You cannot make the rules and break them yourself. Stick to your guns, do not be a copycat or remodel other people's parenting skills. See what works for you and use it, never re-enact your upbringing or else you will keep being in fear of 'familiar Spirits' or family curses.

All is well mum always says

Perhaps all is well

As we are family

That endless live in divine intervention

And supernatural provision

We have solidified ourselves in the root

Of all goodness

And can never ask for a lesser intervention

We pray endlessly for positive outcome

And have purchased mercy in the hands of all supreme

Who can only, identify a solution

And rewrite the act

Staged by Autism

I am being drowned by life uncertainty

As my brother is very unpredictable

He moves from low to high

We all have this nodding dog syndrome

Unsure of answers to life interrogation

We are now embarking on a spiritual journey

And pray it works.

Self -denial

I am a child, remember, but matured in receiving the brutal attacks of life. I have learnt in a hard way and under studied in the strangest manner. If you are looking for someone cajoled into accepting life defeat, I will raise my hand to it. If you are yet to see a child matured into losing her personality I will endorse it. I started denying myself of certain things in life in order to accommodate my brother. Don't get me wrong please, I am not complaining but giving myself a pat on the back. My mum tries as much as possible to ensure we are both enjoying ourselves but when AUTISM strikes it keeps everything at bay. Parenthood for mum is like a journey with several uncertainties but continuous leaning on the one and only who can assure her of a better tomorrow. Sometimes I wish I can elope with mum and have some girly moment but all these are short lived by my brothers Autism. I am not sure what it is, but I know that it is a demon that upsets people and pushes some into resentment, as for me I do not resent my brother but wish things could change for good. I am not going to fully cloth myself with regrets as to what nature should have prevented, but dissect all hidden agenda and find a solution. It is not my fault that I have been born to experience life tyranny but I am always a winner and never loses in life encounter. So therefore I am kicking on the door of life deposits waiting to collect all the collectables. It may not be due to me but I will influence nature's distribution. I am special and that is why life experiences are taking notes from me. I am sure you are yet to encounter someone like me who at my age have threaded the path of Autism and still accomplishes. I have grown to yield myself to all supreme who is faithful and never fails. I know I am born to be the greatest and the most successful regardless of all the intrusions. I am signing myself up for life testimonies knowing full well it will edify most. Sometimes my brother would cry for some more during dinner times as he can eat like a giant. I give him my food, though mum would object and opt to make him more, but I always insist as I feel very happy being extra nice to my brother. I even lost faith in my spirituality as I kept wondering why me. And why should I be created to witness life in its painful mode. It is like life has become infertile clothed with barrenness. It is like the greenery has been invaded with weeds and withered untimely. As time went on life began to shift into my ideology and I started embracing my spirituality. I learnt my lesson about life, that I cannot do anything without leaning on my spiritual wellbeing. It might take a while but it is advisable to wait having a mind-set of – it will surely happen. Sometimes my social life is non-existence due to the fact I had to compromise as mum needs to earn an income. Don't get me wrong I have never missed a pre-arranged outing with friends as mum would always compromise. We as a family have worked as a team and led ambush against all the wickedness of life's mishap. I am glad we are a team and united we stand. I am not sure how mum manages to ensure that none of us lose out on life expectations. We are both lucky to have a very caring mother who never gives up on us. She still manages to distribute her love to other children and family despite her challenges. I am glad I have taking lots of life notes from my mum and wishing and hoping I could tutor others in similar predicament as to what to do. It is not ideal to be reckless or selfish if you are a young carer but learn to carefully, patiently and selflessly deal with every blow life throws at your door step. Sometimes I find myself being bemused by emotional outbursts but had to control myself most times as I am unbearably caught up in this never ending dilemma which I wish could become a satire and I will cloth myself in a hysterical gear. Sometimes mum is worn out by taking care of my brother that she has to rest, and me, being mum's baby would always want attention, but she manages to at least give me some not full.

As I get older, I get more confident and protective of my brother. I see him as my own child that I need to shower with motherly affection, though mother does that already. It is rewarding to care for someone even if they don't show appreciation or know what that means. Most times whenever we visit places we always consider my brother's needs. We try to monitor his response to external stimuli with eagle eye and try as much as possible to avert Autism striking. My world is full of orderliness and sequence. Everything has to be planned, arranged and pre-empted. This is an Autistic world and it goes in array of organised timetable. I sometimes see myself as a robot fascinated by the strangeness of my life routine. We are like an empire being invaded by Autism. The good news is that my mum is the empress and dictates the sequence of events.

Public shame

As I stepped out with my brother we step into the world of prejudice, everyone is looking, everyone is critical. Half of the time no one has a clue as to who my brother is and what is going on with him. Most times he would do something embarrassing to me and to the whole family. Mum is used to accommodating the shame and pretending nothing just transpired. In his younger days it was very awkward and he would sometimes lay on the shop floor and refuse to stand up screaming and shouting. Mum's face would drop in confusion not in shame as to how to get him off the shop floor. People gaze in utmost disrespectful way and I was too young to understand the word, shame or to be impacted, but mum's facial response tells me all is not well. My brother was like a famous person being observed by his fan. We are always like an amusement theme. The whole scenario seems like people where taking life notes at our expense. Tony, the actor, was oblivious of onlookers and their response to his display. 3 days later we were all in the same supermarket, this time Tony was putting stuff in the trolley which was not part of mum's shopping list. As soon as we got to the check out and mum removed the items, he started wailing as if someone was attacking him. I thought mum would be a' push over 'and go ahead and pay for it. She totally ignored the whole tantrum and paid for only what we came for. I guess if mum did pay for it he would have been doing exactly the same thing over and over again if that will earn him a shopping spree. The worst embarrassing moment was when we were in the super market and suddenly people started moving away from us, and that was when Tony was 9 years old. I was about 7 years old and was astounded as to why people were acting strange, suddenly I could smell something really nasty…..it was Tony's poo in his nappy. I was ashamed and prayed no one thought I was responsible for this fowl smelly incident. Mum quickly finished and ordered a cab, as soon as we got in to the car mum ensured the glass was down and almost emptied a bottle of perfume on Tony's trouser. I felt so sorry for mum, things she had to put up with and go through in caring for us. I always have this feeling that my brother's situation was more of a spiritual attack and am praying that the one who created Tony and whom my mum covenanted with from conception will unleash angels to war and destroy the very cause. Sometimes mum would take us out on her Board meetings in 5 star hotels, we still go through the same vicious circle of event though mum always goes with a paid carer. Whenever his nappy is being changed it stunk, the whole room and when he eats the whole dining table was covered with crumbs, mum would walk in and start cleaning, and always mutters 'All is well'. During breakfast time our heart skips as another embarrassing moment was coming. Tony would pick up stuff that fell on the floor from his plate. I just cannot begin to recall these moments because they are huge and play big role in whom, Tony has become now. When Tony was around 9 years old and mum had an interview in the city and needed to drop us off with a friend. We were on the train sitting next to this man who opened his brief case and lined up his lunch. I must say … bad timing. Tony stretched his hand and grabbed the man's crisps; he quickly snatched it off him. This happened repeatedly thrice to be precise until mum apologetically moved Tony. Everyone looked at us in disgust; it looked like mum was a bad mother. I wish I could correct the impression but prayed eagerly for Tony to have a break through. As these disgraceful moments persisted I started gradually losing my confidence but when I got older my spiritual believe revamped the entire personality and made me courageous and confident in whom I am and was created to be. That is not all, my dear. We hardly visit people unless they are close family friends, because they understand my brother. As soon as Tony enters their home, he sits down just like a very good boy. Just give him 10 minutes he runs to their kitchen, look into the cupboard grab what appeals to him, leave it open and walk to the next. This time, the fridge and he will browse through to see what to eat if nothing, he will leave the kitchen with the fridge open. Then he will sit down eating whatever he had found and decorating the floor and chair with crumbs. The house owner at this time was looking very unhappy but curtailed due to mum presence. After eating he will look for any music stereo and play. TAXI!!!!!!!!!! Mum has had enough, she will apologetically close the cupboard and the fridge, sweep the floor and switch off the music. At this point our host is relaxed and a lot more accommodating, but it is time to go. That does it Tony!!!!! Even though I love going out, I will be forced not to visit anyone's home anymore. The good lesson is if we must go, we take along with us a packed lunch, CD player with ear phone and that has been saving us from unwelcoming gestures.

When you observe my routine in my younger days you will understand the strength that we young carers have, it must have been ordained from birth. I am perplexed as to the way nature turned against me and my folks as if we are wrapped around ice waiting to melt, it is morbidly isolating due to the ailment....Autism. Don't feel sorry for me but I want you to find comfort in my pain and solace in my hurt. Even when we are on holidays, it is as if we just moved home, but still doing exactly the same thing, as Autism has refused mum rest. I have this assurance that mum too will not allow Autism a moment of rest too.

Mum is actually special not sure how she swaps between moods in other to make us happy. It is worrisome how some people are always having the best of life beauty while others are drowning in most ugly situation. I am a giant on top of all the world craziness and its brethren yet am managing to downsize to the utmost level of subtleness. I have been pushed so hard up to the level of no return by life wickedness but I manage to look in the mirror and find my future unhampered. I know that I am equipped with wings and can reach heights thanks to the quest imposed by autism. It takes me to wake up and find my life in twist and still manage to loosen up and give happy cheers to my obstacle. Please don't think I am moaning, I am only pouring out my heart in order to assist you in coping with life predicaments. I am an expert in life Autism mishap and would like to hold your hand and accompany you to the seat of 'overcomers' where I and my family are proudly seated.

Loneliness

You will not understand what loneliness is, until you walk in the shoes of the lonely. The world might be generous to offer you lots of people but nothing significant. I am not the only child sometimes it seems so. My brother is transfixed into this lonesome corner, which is his scared space. No one can interrupt his moment of self-idolised time, where and when he is sunken into the world of 'me' and myself. I feel abandoned and left to find solace in mum or my friends. It is unfair but they say nothing is fair, as far as I know and care everything is designed and scripted by life director to be fair. Even though ailments like Autism have stolen the script of life from most; but still the script of life can never be erased. Do not fret my friend, but command your stage to be set as planned, then the whole life script will follow suit. I have played with inanimate objects so much that I dislike them with passion, as life drama has taken my dearest brother off my script as an active actor and have resorted in making him an effigy. Sometimes I want to just concentrate on friendship but it never satisfies; like your own blood that can never let you down, other times, to mum who tries to be my sister, but sometimes it goes wrong. As I struggle to maintain mother and daughter respect. It is a serious drama mum is good in switching roles as my friend, sister and mum. But I struggle, even though she is my confidant. I wonder how the only child of the family copes, perhaps better than me, as life from start have conditioned them in that singular position. I accept the fact life gets very imaginative sometimes as I am used to creating my companion. Well, it is good I love studying and that gets me out of life chaos and occupies my time. My house can be quiet really quiet, you can even hear a pin drop and a curtain drawn. In the similitude of all these life events I resort to directing myself to divert to my internal companion ordained from start. It is overwhelming to stand and keep standing in all these life dramas without stooping. Sometimes I wonder how I have grown without being stunted by life prejudice. I am dazzled by the fact that I am disjointed by my conjoined twin the dilemma of Autism that is why I am a victorious warrior. The pillar of life has resolved in keeping me still and steady, I am surely thankful for being acquainted with him the one that keeps me sane and focused despite the insanity and chaos of life. I am definitely lonesome shielded by the self-interrogation of had it been, had it been my brother was normal then I will be with company most times. But that might not be case, sometimes you can be in the midst of ocean and die of thirst. Who am I to audition life characters and apportion them to act accordingly? When the door of my room is shut I am forced to rely on indwelling companion to accompany me to the gallery of life where only my thoughts are displayed.

My Brother at present

He has really grown into a remarkable handsome young man.....well done mum and thank you God. He is settled in his new college and has acquired new skills; he has been able to do work experiences too. His self harming episode has decreased. Mum took a lot of drastic measures like having sensory lights at home and black out curtain. No more yogurts, but less dairy product for breakfast. No more harmonica and keyboards as we have identified that sounds and certain music increase his self harming episode, Things have changed between us since the last book in 2014, he no longer wants my company instead he commands me to go upstairs to my room and when he comes to my room he commands me to sit on the chair or bed whichever he prefers. I am not happy with this new development, but I know why? Since I started my A 'levels I have been extremely busy academically and have resort to being in my room all the time so he got used to the fact that room is my space and when I now want to come down more often he is finding it very awkward and confusing. This Autism is a very strange ailment as siblings of young people with the diagnosis we cannot be dismayed but try to adjust to the demands of life until things get better. I am optimistic they will surely move away from the manipulation of the ailment. I wish you all the best in all your life pursuit take care, I love you lots. xx

CHAPTER 12

Time for Love

Nobody loves you more than you, if you do not love yourself you can never visualise love in anything, neither will you be willing to show love. Even when you see it or even shown love the retrospect is that no one can love you in your situation.

Sometimes you let yourself be trodden under foot by others because you feel in your situation you owe the world a duty or you feel you have to pay a price to be loved as your situation calls for sympathy. My dear, you are a princess fully crowned and clothed in royal garment, parade yourself as one and do not allow anyone, at any time, to make you feel worthless. You have something special which no one has, and that special thing sets you apart, builds your character and integrity. You are one of a kind, a unique extraordinary person created to carry the grace of love and compassion. You might shed tears and be sad at times but in that solemn moment is a time for you to receive and observe the divine overwhelming mercy, grace, and the warmth of his compassionate love. Like my uncle always advises me—do not shop around for men, let them hunt you down. Men seek women and find them, women are given opportunity to either accept or reject. These days, things are different; the value of female specie has fallen tremendously. Like Beyoncé said if you like it put a ring on it, but women are too scared to give men such options. Lots of men needed to test the product first before putting their money on it. I cry sometimes, you know, not that I am hurting inside but the unkind, uncaring, selfish, and ignorant attitude people I come across display. People want to plunge into your life using your situation to use and abuse your kindness. When you are in this situation that is when you can know who exactly cares for you and who wants to use you. I have learnt that wickedness lies deeply in the heart of man and man has pervasive urge to indulge in wickedness. I tried relationships after I broke up from my children's dad, or perhaps I should say relationships tried me because they come to me, I don't go to them. The ideal person I thought was someone who can love my son and help me with his care and support. I was not looking for love or trying to be loved. I ended up meeting people with very low self-esteem, no self-actualisation and psychologically and emotionally messed up. They were like leeches, blood-sucking vampires ready to suck you spiritually, materially, emotionally, and physically dry. I needed someone to help me but ended up with people who were so emotionally and materially dependent on me. They never thought for a second that I have a child with special needs and I needed lots of care and affection. They manipulated my situation using my son as an icon to encourage their lousy lifestyle. Human beings are so cruel and crude they feel that you ought to pay them for the company and their heart seems not to prick for their disheartening act of deceit. Everyone wants something and no one seems to give without getting anything in return.

If you are reading this book and you are wondering why I keep meeting the same type of people. The reason is that I keep lowering my standards because I feel the lower they are, the more likely they can adjust to assisting me with my son.

No way girlfriend! These men are but pieces of trash that needs to be trashed. They say the good ones are already taken and those still hanging around must be carrying loads!!!! And truly my friend, I am a witness and can testify. People that have been single for a while cannot wait to be hooked up and those hooked up already cannot wait to be unhooked. I suppose life predisposes us to desire what you need and are yet to receive. People have the impression that as a parent with special needs child the government is filling your bank account with millions of money and perhaps they lack nothing but a man to assist them in spending the money. I have spoken to parents of these children who happen to be vulnerable because of their situation in caring for their children as lone parents. They meet men and women including family members and friends who walk into their lives pretending to be the best carers in the universe but end up being nightmares. If you are a woman in any vulnerable state do not befriend a man who you can assist in anyway but someone who can contribute to your life. Girlfriend, write down what you desire from your ideal man and run with it, do not underestimate what you can find do not lower your standard or compromise. Frankly speaking I did not need to be in any relationship as I was able myself; they were just mere time wasters and ignorant folks. Like I mentioned, at the peak of your vulnerability men who are lazy and idle will creep into your household because you are already susceptible to fall for men who can care for your children. The mistake we carers make is that we act in a vulnerable manner. Once any foolish person shows the slightest inclination that they care for our children we throw in the towel. Ladies be careful, most of the male specie who can entice vulnerable women because of what they need from them are evil— excuse my language, just be careful. Don't pay his bills, give him money, or settle his immigration status. You are worth more than what you think, don't cut love corners, ensure you meet someone who can make you happy, be selfish for once look for a man who is loaded with cash and intellect. What's wrong with that?

CHAPTER 13

Caring

Caring depicts loving and loving is caring.

You care because you need and love to care

But you love to care as the person you care for

Is the object of the love, which is born out of selflessness and love

Caring is a unique duty rewarding, but demanding.

We care because we love to care

The love we have spurs us to care some more.

A person who cares has the personality of a personal angel whose wings is glued to their heart.

They would love to fly someday to greater heights to respond to their future but can't, as the caring role decides their response to life external stimuli.

A Carer is made; no one is born to function in the role

But created with special characteristics to create enablement

Life inevitable also designs you in the role as if custom made

Care changes our perception of life and for the proud amongst us it enforces humility and patience.

Caring is a very rewarding thing to do, but you may never get an acknowledgment or thank you from your client or child.

Some care because they love to care and others care because there is a need to care and no one else can function in the role

Some care in pain and regrets, others care with love and prayer

I love my son and love to care and care to care.

He is worth caring for and worth showering with love.

Though sometimes he is unpredictable, yet my love predicts the situation and enhances my role to care with confidence.

Sometimes I am low but the height comes when my motherly instincts is ignited into my soul and injects its beauty of motherhood.

It spurs me into visualising the angelic vision of conceiving him

This makes me smile and smile.

Sometimes I am weak but the heavenly stand-up ovation

And applaud to my role, quickens my inner being.

As I am human and need a jump start at times, this enables me to rise up to the occasion destiny has called me to rise up, bounce back and pronounce my unquestionable willingness to care and care with love.

I am determined to fight the battle of caring for my son and to become a voice that will speak his inner thought and desire so loud and clear.

As life has put a demand on me to care, even at adulthood, yet I would independently ensure that he is independent enough to be independent.

As he is young and agile, full of vigour and vitality.

I will try as much as possible to ensure that my caring will not inhibit his ability to be independent, but enhance his ability not diminish him to total dependency and reliance on my care.

CHAPTER 14

Life and the Carer

When you encounter people who say they rather have it one way or the other, I always say to people, it is not about your choices and desires. It is all about mercy and grace hoping that fortune follows or crosses our path. Do you ever wonder why you do not have a say to certain things in life, perhaps if you do you will become a miniature god and ascribe all glory and power to yourself. Humans are now trying to make choices as to the type of children they will have through choices made in sperm banks. No matter how fascinating and fantastic our choices are, they cannot prevent certain ailment in our lives. I saw a beautiful baby pop out of my womb with no birth defects. I did not know few years later he could have AUTISM, never, say never. They say but for those of us who are firm believers would say that hope in God changes everything. Life might put undue pressures in our expectancies but the spirit of God inside assures us of a waiting time and accomplishing period. The mind of every human being is always in a desperate mood—we want it, we want it now without weighing the pros and cons. I know now but I don't know any second from now. Life is so unpredictable and our faith and hope of a great future empowers us to withdraw from untimely anxiety. There is nothing unearthing about life, the more you dig into it the more you get drowned without any answers. If man was to shop for children in the supermarket we may still not check out with the best. We might be impulsive as to make wrong choices or perhaps our financial resources might debar us from getting what we want and at the time we want it. Life is an institution and every stage is a teacher we, the students, sometimes pass or fail the examination life gives us. People who learn always succeed in life tests, while those who are nonchalant end up repeating mistakes all over again. When issues knock on your door you are expected to let them in but how you handle them is entirely up to you because once at the door it becomes inevitable. When I saw autism coming, hardly did I know I needed a helmet to protect me from the impending knock on effect on my family's wellbeing? You do not need to be cajoled into accepting autism, it is an ailment unhidden and unmasked hence the reason most parents diagnose their children before medical practitioners. It has an impact not just to the victim but anyone that crosses their path. It is intense, dramatic and unpredictable, the more you look the less you see, the further you eavesdrop the less likely you hear. I can only stand to salute carers of any kind whether to friends, families, spouses, and employees. It is a role that calls for intense inhibition but very rewarding, we need to take pride in this life journey though unprepared but the destination will justify the journey. Most of us are nature converts brought together by nature's mishap. It is our duties to ensure we evangelise with the tools nature has deposited in us. Sometimes it is uncertain to precisely denote nature's intention but we are influenced by the traumatic episodes that nature has casually orchestrated to prostrate before us and casually land on our feet. Life is interesting and we are the trumpeters announcing the forbidden entrance of nature's mishap. I, for one, would step aside and allow the person that knows best my spiritual guardian to dissuade, deploy, and divert all the assigned nature's hazard not my way but back to wherever it might have come from.

Rewriting Autism

Yes, they might say he or she has autism but what do you think? What is your inner conviction telling you? You can rewrite a child's destiny and capture the inner abilities of your child which no one can ever see or know but you. I have seen children diagnosed with autism go to universities and work. Please do not allow your child to go to a special needs primary school but encourage them in mainstream unless it is obvious that they have learning difficulties or are clinically diagnosed mute. No child is actually mute; it is a decision they make to be mute. You need to encourage your child to speak by rewarding speech, show them that speaking is invaluable and very rewarding. To get what you want you need to communicate what you want. Otherwise, you will not get what you want, the choice is theirs.

We, parents, are fighters and I would advise you to fight to win and be positive to inflict change through research and studies. I pray that your eye of understanding will be focused on the solution rather than the problem. Pretend there is no one out there until you get an adequate prescription. Chin up, girlfriend. Thank God autism is not a life sentence, once there is life there is hope.

CHAPTER 15

If Only He Can

I f only Tony could explain what, where, how, and who
then I will be taking a deep breath of satisfaction. I can
only hope and believe that wherever he is, he is safe. If
Tony can defend himself then I would joyfully envisage that
he will cope with daily prejudices. If only Tony can tell the
doctor the location of his pain, then his cure will be hastened.
If only Tony can express his emotional needs, then there will
not be any need for him to cry. If only Tony can tell me how
he feels about his self-esteem and the unrealistic nature of
his getting to that level, then he will no longer be flapping his
hand in anxiety. If only Tony can scream sometimes then I
will know the state of his emotions and what his needs are.
If only Tony can express his fears and anxiety, then he will
no longer rock his head back and forth. If and if only Tony
will have counselling sessions to discuss what is going on in
his mind perhaps there will not be any need for him to hit
himself to exert pain. If Tony can be empowered to discover
his potential, then I would pay anything for a life coach.

Sometimes we all need to cry and a little cry here and there is a
healthy option that will not clog our heart and system. When
we cry, it seems so normal, but if a person with autism with
limited communication and social difficulty cries, it becomes
an unscripted act or socially unacceptable or a misnomer.

Maybe I should say perhaps a matter of apologising for being different. If only Tony can express the impact of daily living and interaction with people, then there will not be any need to carry the tag—autism and the emblem—I am different. Life demand on every one is insurmountable regardless of your ability or disability we all need to empty the guile of existing with others in order to make sense of existence and come out fulfilled. If only Tony can express the riotous hormonal war going on within, then I will no longer have need to play the guessing game. Though autistic, he has hormonal issues which he internalises without any external input making it look more like a psychopathic episode. Professionals make assumptions as to the similitude the ailment with other illnesses as if the tag autism is not enough. Tags are placed by owners to identify their products and to give information to others, but autism as a tag is neither placed by the owner nor is it used as awareness but a term that makes the bearer socially diminished and defaced.

CHAPTER 16

Playing a Father's Role

I just remembered walking into the church on father's day and saying to Pastor Ben, 'happy father's day', and he said to me, 'happy father's day too'. I was surprised and dismayed I looked back and he said, 'you are a father, too, my sister, you are a father.'

Interesting concept, perhaps I am not, on gender basis but identified and prescribed role by nature. His dad, bless him, is part of his life but cannot commit much as he has his own family, too and lived outside the country, God is good.

I was just wondering maybe I should have called this book being Tony's mum and dad. Playing both roles seems very interesting for women especially having to cut his hair and shave his beard. Tony hates the vibration from the shaver so does most children diagnosed with Autism. I use to sit him down, hold him or get his sister to hold him, while I shave him. If Tony goes to the barber it will take at least four men to hold him to shave his hair. It is intriguing to visualise his sister holding him to have a haircut and how he allows her to hold him while I cut his hair, my thought to that effect is due to trust, love, and being fond of his sister. This was before he turned 14 years old and was around 5'12" whilst his sister was just less than 4ft.

Now he is older and much bigger and the good thing is that he can sit nicely for anyone to give him a nice razor comb shaving. He allows electric shaver from time to time but not close to his ears or where he can feel the vibration. I do his cloth and shoe shopping which I enjoy doing, I forgot to tell you my secret, I use to be a tomboy when I was growing up and admire male outfits, I felt they were cute. But now, I am supper girly and love dressing up but still have time to go into male clothing shops to pick out the best and the latest for my son. I learnt to shave him perfectly to avoid razor bumps. The good thing is that he has the perfect skin that is not prone to razor bump. My secret is a very good brand of shaving stick, Dettol, and use nappy rash cream after shaving. This keeps the bump at bay. When he had to go to prom I dressed him up, bought him a suite, trouser, and waist coat. My son looked very princely and dapper in the outfit, not just an ordinary prince but a charming one. My son is currently 6'2" and I just wonder how I have been coping taking care of a big man whilst I am just 5'4". I can only say but for God and motherly attachment which makes a giant dwarf and ogre tender. My mum says mothers love is never done, you keep being a mother until you take the last breath, but we don't know whether the role continues in the other realm . . . who knows, if the mother continues as a spiritual guardian and mentor. No matter where the role starts and ends it is important that we ensure we play our part to the best of our knowledge. My mum always uses this Ibo adage *'when you want to eat a toad ensure it is the fat one, so that when people call you a toad eater, you can comfortably and boldly sanction your role'*. This means that, what is worth doing is worth doing well. I

did not stumble into caring role by chance or happenstance
but life scripted the role for me to play without consent and
I ensure that I act to the audience's approval.

CHAPTER 17

Self-harming

It is well known fact that some people diagnosed with autism self-harm. What exactly is self-harming? Self-harm is when somebody intentionally damages or injures their body. People with autism self-harm as a means of coping with stress or expressing overwhelming emotional distress. Self-harming for a child with autism has an anesthesia–like effect where by the person feels numbness to pain and also endorphins are released into their system bringing about a feeling of content or relief or should I say a kick like feeling. After so many years of caring for my son I began to understand why people with autism self-harm, it is because their threshold of pain is minimal. When he starts hitting himself he does not feel pain but at some point he moves from wailing to proper crying, if you observe him you will notice that he is getting more emotional from the pain. I just cannot fathom what makes him hit himself like a boxer in a ring; even boxers wear protective clothing to combat the degree of impact. Tony was never inclined to self-harming until he turned 14 years old and I wish I understood events that mediated such an act. The trigger factor sometimes is obvious and sometimes I play guessing game which is pivotal to my caring role as his mum to enable me to identify and deal with reoccurrences. Some ignorant people felt he must have a mental health issue for him to be self-harming but I always say it is within the autistic spectrum and being heavily built does not make some people accommodating of the situation. Sometimes I just wish I can sooth the pain or make things better, watching your son go through pain is like a vivid description of one's child being attacked by a gang, though he is doing the attack. Sometimes I wish I can say to autism, 'Listen, autism, it is about time we confront each other. I have fought you physically, psychologically, emotionally, spiritually, and it is about time you throw the towel in or put up a challenge.' I am still exploring and investigating the cause of this unscrupulous ailment and in the process of my research I decided to explore these possible causations, perhaps I could attribute it to the following: a seizure, which an EEG scan can identify. It is known as electroencephalography, a neurological test that uses an electronic monitoring devise to measure and record electrical activity in the brain. Irritable bowel syndrome which is a disorder of the interaction between the brain and gastrointestinal tract and people diagnosed with autism tend to have abnormalities in the gut. I have managed to remove yogurt and dairy products from his daily intake. Perhaps he might have lactose intolerance like me, but that did not work. One thing I have noticed is the days that he has more binging, the more he tends to have crying outbursts. The less he eats the more settled he tends to adjust during the day. He is a teenager, he has flesh and blood flowing in his veins, and he has hormones too, just like every male. How he copes with this hormonal battle I don't know. Perhaps it is internalised and comes out as an emotional outburst. He is human, too, he goes through pain and anxiety about life;

he also desires to function normally and do things his mates do. How can an ignorant person attribute such feelings to psychopathic episodes? If he is opportune to lie on the couch with a shrink and able to express his feelings, then people will understand how this young man feels and what he is going through. He knows life has built block and clusters around him which he wants to pull down but finds it difficult to as he lacks the necessary communication tools to have a dialogue with life and destroy all the obstructions. Ability to withstand pain is not just an autistic thing, if you have been traumatised by life predicaments you will understand and have the capacity to assimilate pain. Frankly speaking, pain has become me or perhaps I have become pain. Every hour, minutes, and seconds is like your body goes into an expectant mode, awaiting pain in any form and by the time you know it you are immune to withstand pain. Show me a person who has seen pain inflicted on another, yet you have no choice to interfere, or a person who has been crushed by life expectancies, then I will introduce myself. Yet by His grace I stand tall not willing to be dwarfed. If no one is ready to give me applaud or standup ovation, I will commend myself for a diamond medal. This commendation is not just for me but also for all the parents and significant others of children with autism; I salute you for all your effort.

I have seen it all, I have heard it all and experienced all yet my encounter with life is not pitiful but challenging. I have grown with pain and I no longer exhibit emotions because I no longer can, but can weep for others who are going through similar situation. I am now like an animal being aimed at by the hunter yet chewing gum or puffing cigar. I am like one facing her executioner yet blowing a trumpet of victory. I am like a dwarf that put up a basketball challenge with a giant. I am all the impossible yet I have undoubtedly excelled, optimistic that these challenges are building me to become and to achieve the impossible. Don't cry for me, folks, for life loves me so much as to allow me to be exposed to autism and have an opportunity to raise a special child with great expectations. I decided to read up extensively on self-harming and autism. In the process of my research and investigation I picked up the following which I started using and doing to him. I bought sensory lights from Argos and I use mirrors. These sensory lights I use them in my living room and his room in the evenings and the mirrors I use when he is self-harming to show him what he does to himself. This seems to be working, thank God, let me not talk too soon, they say the walls have ears and evil people inhabit those walls. (Laugh out loud).

Tony expectations

It is painful to be me

And reassuring to have a mum like mine

I am not sure what pain is any longer

And what it feels like

I have experienced rejections

And no longer expect acceptance

I am a victim of life defects

And a reject of life idealism

I don't have expectation

But I have short comings

That is becoming my identity

I am an onlooker unsure

Life ventures intentions

I am living and relying on others for existence

I exist under the canopy of others

Waiting to be fully sheltered

I pray regularly for a miracle

That will rewrite life expectations

And handover my expectations

Without undue pressures

I am waiting to be clothed in impossibilities

And achieve the impossible.

Possibly I will be dancing a victorious lullaby

To life predicament

I am living and entrusting

My entire existence on others

Not knowing when and how they will turn against me.

Every day, every minute, every hour

I am harnessed in making people's desire mine

Yet I believe I have mine

Mine which seems rather non existence

Perhaps one day,

I am confident that I will not permanently

Be deterred from achieving my rightful right

I will one day walk in and collect what belongs to me

And watch life predicaments be dethroned by my expectations

Which will surely happen?

But when, am not sure.

But surely will happen

Filter or Delete

I am beginning to understand why my son was constantly self-harming; he was struggling with over stimulating environmental factors. As normal as some of us claim to be we can chose to delete or filter information, but someone with autism find it difficult to do that. That is why at some point they reach their information overload stage and they burst into tears and self harming. It must be very frightening to be aware of your mind and brain interaction. We all do get strange suggestions in our mind but we don't carry them out, but people with autism find it difficult to reject demands imposed by the mind through suggestions. Learn to assist your child to filter and delete information it will go a long way to help them curb self harming episodes.

CHAPTER 18

Age Appropriate Stuff

Now Tony is going to be 20 in May, what should his hobby be? What is the age appropriate play for him? What does a typical adult do? Well, well, watch MTV, 18 rated movies, drink and smoke, evangelise, chat up girls, parties, play games, mobile phone obsession, and try out stuff that adults do. Some might, at this point, explore their sexual awareness and see how far they can go. In some extreme cases, have become a baby father or been in and out of prison. The world is not enough and neither sufficient, life does not have the capacity for optimal but equilibrium and mostly imbalance. People tend to put up a brave face to suggest they have arrived and everything is wonderful, yet there is a glimpse of uncertainty and in completeness somewhere, though, might be hidden. My son loves watching cartoons like *Sponge Bob Square Pants*, Scooby Doo, and anything in cartoon form. This is not age appropriate but where do you draw the line and when do you say to him that's it and how do you convey the message for him to understand he is too old to be stuck in a child's world. If Michael Jackson was alive he might like to make my son his best buddy just like Peter Pan, maybe supervised contact due to child protection or safeguarding concerns. (Laugh out loud). I love Michael though, not sure of the unproven allegation regarding child abuse, perhaps they are truth that has gone with him to the grave. I guess what we enjoy doing is based on individual preferences, not how we have been brought up. People argue that lack of nurturing makes people to be permanently children. I tell you my son is over nurtured and it makes no difference. He watches normal films from time to time but I had to make sure they are PG, nothing more. He loves MTV but under my supervision he can watch it. Tell you what, sometimes MTV can be X rated, due to prevalent sexual explicit acts. These young men do not have the capacity to understand some sexual connotation and acts so why expose them to it. Some carers who work in homes talk about young people who masturbate in public, oblivious of onlookers. They say little drops of water make up an ocean so why engage these kids in things you cannot control. I am one of those parents who do not tolerate a child playing with his private parts. You, as a parent, from the beginning need to infer the magnitude of such behaviour or else you will not control it when the child gets older. Do not make inappropriate romantic or sexual gestures with your husband or partner in front of these children. Do not assume that since they have learning difficulty they are unable to deduce what is happening around them. I have heard people on talk shows and books advise that masturbation is good, I say it is psychologically, spiritually, and emotionally wrong, more so can be damaging this is my opinion, not enforced. The act shows lack of self-control and indiscipline. God did not create human for sex act nor sex act create for human to explore indiscriminately but an act for procreation. Teach your child the right things that will assist them in life and they will not depart from it. The fact that your child is diagnosed with autism or has learning difficulty does not mean they have moral difficulty, it is our duty to instil discipline and deter inappropriate act. Parents who have children with Asperger allow them to go online unsupervised or without parental lock. The mind of a child is very curious and explores at any moment in time. It is better to be safe than sorry, a little no, you can't, here and there will not kill anyone perhaps few tears but preserve their sanity. My son loves listening to music, playing his keyboard and harmonica. He enjoys singing and like me, usually off key. His hobby is very descent and I encourage it. He plays on his tablet and mobile phone. When he was younger I discourage him from playing with his private part and he does not do that, he knows it is very wrong and people frown at such act. These young men are still virgins and what you don't know will not hurt you, it is only when they are or have been tampered with that they become uncontrollable. They say that they don't have the capacity to be married or marry but when it comes to encouraging them to have sex, they have the capacity. Marriage legally is not consummated without sexual relationship so technically sex connotes marriage. How hypocritical if they are not allowed to marry why are they allowed to have sex, or we are living in a perverted generation were illicit sex is permissible but marriage is not.

There are so many interesting things to keep these young people occupied and enjoy life and sexual act is the least. He assists me with household chores like plugging the vacuum cleaner, toasting bread, putting clothes in washing machine, putting plates in the sink, emptying plates in the bin, carrying heavy manly item, and many others.

CHAPTER 19

What Does Safeguarding
Mean For Us

Autism is a disability that impacts on all aspect of your wellbeing both for the victim and the family. Most people at an early stage misunderstand what is going on in the child's life. Sometimes people use punishment as a measure to combat bad behaviour thinking that solution will come. A typical child with autism is unruly as described by outsiders and it goes beyond the ethics of proper upbringing, the more you try the worse it seems to become. The alarm blows like a war signal without any third party, you and your son are in the battle and the silent enemy is trying to trash your relationship to pieces. These children are innocent and victims of circumstance of birth defect. Some families see themselves as victims and the child the problem, please; I would like you to have a rethink. It is rare to find social services taking children with autism away from home rather some parents are willing to give them away as they no longer can cope with daily demands. The question is how do you know when a child with autism is being neglected? They bite, scratch, fight, tear, cut, dirty themselves, and abusive to themselves. They are already children in need but how does the social worker ascertain that they have graduated from that to the care of the community and raise concern.

Autism, just like mental health, has limited attention due to the nature. There have been situations where these children have been killed by family members in the past due to lack of support. I would advise that once a diagnosis of autism is made, a child should compulsorily be registered as a child in need and the children with disabilities team should work with the family to ensure they have support and can cope. The only time social services step in is when there is need for direct payment, housing, exclusion or transition to adulthood. These children are vulnerable and it is vital that the social services incorporate their welfare as being paramount. We have watched media highlights vulnerable people being abused by carers in care homes, has someone ever wondered what happens to children with autism when the doors are shut and darkness takes control of light. We hear Baby P, Victoria Climbie, and many other children who are victims of adult brutality and callousness, how many children with autism have been relevant to the statistics. I am very passionate about children and vulnerable people and believe the society owe them a duty to assist, support, and protect them from harm and danger. They have already been short changed by life so why don't we enable them to gain from existence. These children, whether we like it or not, are the future of the universe, be it aspergers, autism or conduct disorder. They are all precious vessels in God's sight that can shine as long as we ignite them with love. Children with autism lack communication skills that can enable them to adequately confirm life mistrust, they lack a social skill that deter their ability to function in a universe so demanding, so sensitive, and reads meaning from every movement regardless of the intention. These children go to school and no one conducts an inspection or a regulatory body is put in place to ensure that they are not abused. The issue here is that they are proclaimed abusers themselves so how, when, where do we confirm what is actually going on. I hope you understand the predicaments these children go through, I do as a mother of one for over 19 years going to 20 years. He is the most loving person I have come across he can never ever hurt a fly. Despite all that, he has been in a position where people have exaggerated or said untrue stuff about him. I, as his voice, had to stand in the gap and speak for him, the cruelty of mankind has indeed no boundaries, the fact life has left you with lack does not prevent people from stealing from you. The mind of man is dangerous and thinks nothing but evil, it takes divine encounter to be purged from it all. The average human is selfish, wanting and needing to acquire and exploit, selflessness can only come from a heart touched and purified. If someone comes up to you to say I am changed, please find out the encounter behind the change otherwise you will be entrusting your life to an enemy who may or may not know he is one. I hope and pray that things will change in the social services and these children will become paramount and MATTER to the society they exist in.

CHAPTER 20

Autism and Exorcism

Most people with learning difficulty have emotional outbursts, rage, or fits whatever you choose to call it. The fact that they are unable to communicate appropriately is the most frustrating factor. I guess the person reading this book cries sometimes and feel like hitting your head on the wall sometimes. The difference between you and Tony is that you have the capacity to make choices regarding the response to your emotions. The fact that my emotions are weighing me down does not mean I am hallucinating or having psychopathic moment. You see people commit suicide, jump on the train lines and moving vehicle. These are people who can no longer contain the weight of life predicaments but believe that ending their life will end the nagging issues of life. Please pause for a minute, take a deep breath and think of seconds, minutes, days, months, and years that you felt so disheartened about life, that you feel that you need an exit to life challenges. I use to attribute everything to spirituality; at some point I felt my son's issue was an attack from a negative force. A friend of mine took me to a church to perform deliverance from evil force. On getting there, I was advised to take my son home not to bring him there, to prevent him from being attacked by demons. Interesting, the message I got from all these is that a prayerful, knowledgeable, and optimistic mother is a tool that can combat any force whether human, spiritual, psychological, or emotional. Please don't misunderstand me, without prayers I will not have had a backbone to resist. I am one of those that depend on God for everything without Him, I am nothing. I will tell you my encounter early hours of the morning with autism.

I just finished an encounter as I write this at 3.44 a.m., I am still awake praying and hoping he sleeps. My son just had an attack; he had been okay until I sent him to bed. Like I said earlier, in the previous chapter, autism is not an ailment otherwise it would have a cure, it is a demon that oppresses household and innocent victims. It is so subtle and sneaky and knows when to attack. I just cannot begin to fathom how these attacks come about; it is like an unexpected blow that keeps the observer in state of commotion until it settles. I am one of those blessed parents because my son is naturally very passive, perhaps if he had been active and aggressive I would end up with bruises, scratches, and bites. The painful thing is that he does that to himself. Some researchers call these 'night terrors' and I don't understand what they are. I was eager and willing to confront these terrors if any but none. I prayed for him, held his hand, and removed his sweat-soaked top, ensuring he is dressed suitably for bed. Sometimes he requests for water and I give it to him it tends to be soothing but what soothes more is the voice of a loving caring mother. My son might have disability but he understands the voice of the wicked and can withstand from afar, he knows the face of cruelty and gives an emotional outburst, he understands pain and avoids it, he feels the presence of evil people and avoids their interaction.

CHAPTER 21

My Son the Gentleman

Please allow me to introduce monsieur Tony. He is a gentleman, captivating and touching everyone he encounters. He is like an angel without wings but flies beyond recognition to halt the heart of wickedness. He is caring and takes on any household works as instructed; he does not argue or complain. Tony is always happy and puts on a smile regardless of what is going on within and outside him. He paints the walls around the home in diverse colourful shades which depicts his anxiety. He is a child of destiny and his presence is full of empowerment. Tony Is full of love though he may not say much but his aura signifies the inbuilt goodness. He may not say thank you to me but the warmth of his personality expresses his gratitude though most of the time he does. He uses the word 'please' and 'thank you' as if it was inscripted in him from conception. He is not aggressive but passive and sees the universe as a place of calm. He is peaceful and enjoys His Company. He understands and knows what it takes to be good and goes out of his way to be. He reads me like a book and understands my emotions more than anyone else. He is very sensitive not because of his sensory needs but he knows the meaning to all my facial gestures and that makes him know my approval in all things. He may not be able to sweep a woman off her feet by many words but his silence is enough to move you. He is and will be the desire of a young lady who wants the best for herself for Tony is the best. He is pure, untainted, and uncanny the more you look the less you are able to unravel his weakness. In fact, he has no weakness and the capability to be weak. Maybe I would say he lacks ability but not that he has a fault. He is nature's wonder harnessed in a tag. He is a champion in the making hidden by disability. His choice of words is pure though unlimited. He is kind and draws your attention to misdeeds. He is a power in a sachet yet to be unleashed. He is a voice that the universe is waiting and yet to hear. He is a prince and his throne is within the confinement of his person and his crown in the heart of those who love him dearly. He is a magnet of goodness and virtue and attracts the pure. He is light ignited to create a path of favour for his family. He is a treasure hidden in the chest of the wicked but one day, he will be hunted and exhibited in the showcase where he belongs. He is a joy not yet exploding into laughter but limited by life expectations. His horse gallops into the heart of the impossible and unearthing its content. He is created to unmake the made works of the wicked. Though bound by boundaries of autism, he is an army unlimited by the present siege. I call him a giant not because of his physical attributes but the height of the impending accomplishments. I know that I know he will be celebrated by life regardless of life choices, his maker has endorsed it and so shall it be. He is uncommon but spectacular with spectators awaiting him to be ushered in. The grand finale is that Tony will be what God has orchestrated from time.

CHAPTER 22

Reality of existence

Having Tony has revealed the wickedness and cruelty of mankind and the true meaning of love. I am glad that I am a fame believer of the existence of the Supreme Being—the God of the universe who orchestrates life events without whom there won't and there can't be no matter what and how we try. Having him has made me a strong person and an inbuilt stamina to expel every uncertainty and pessimism. I am a tool in the hand of the creator and he has got the remote control and He decides which station I channel my whole being to. Let me be honest with you whether you believe in anything or not, perhaps you believe in scientology or evolution and that there is no supreme being. One thing we both can agree on at this point is that you are just a passenger in life transportation—the driver decides where your destination is and how you get there. Your belief or lack of one does not change the fact that you have no say. As a mother your child is your responsibility and no one else's, as for others they are onlookers awaiting the onset of life struggles perhaps to assist or ridicule the situation. Life is about choices; you either chose to adjust to what life has invited unannounced to your home or lose track of life agenda without which you end up dysfunctional. I am versatile with life pros and cons and have been able to deduce what to do to minimise the pain. The philosophical view about life is just enjoying the ride regardless of the destination. I am not interested in the destination, but my relationship with the driver which might digress nature's hazard. We all desire to go to paradise when we exit the universe but no one wants to exit yet, maybe that is why most people don't like challenges. I have reached a level where people might consider me to have seen and experienced all. I will correct you at this point, I have seen and experienced less than most but I trumpet mine. They say a closed mouth is a closed destiny so who am I to keep quiet, when natures issues have not kept silent. No one can handle your case more seriously than you, you know where and how it hurts. No one can be entrusted to act on your child's behalf than you, you are the little god that he feels decides his destiny. Every child needs an attachment and when you, as the attaché, withdraw yourself from the service of parenthood or representation then you have completely disappointed your appointee who has entrusted you to care for these ones. Sir or madam, your responsibility is vital to the society and you are expected to combat chaos. Life is becoming so uncertain and our children are epitome of nature's anxiety, we need to support them through love and care to make this world a safe place for them to be in.

CHAPTER 23

Can Tony Fall in Love?

The legislation has instructed Tony that he is incapable of making marital choices. He has eye and can see the beautiful ladies that God has created. Young ladies gaze at him sometimes and make flirtatious gestures, but my son is wrapped and engaged in his own world to relate to such. He is handsome and very gentle and he has the entire physical attribute to die for but for the cognitive, social, and communication skills debarred by autism. They say love is blind perhaps one day he will create butterfly flutters in the heart of a young woman or make her heart beat abnormally. Like I said earlier in the previous chapters, I dedicated my son to God's service as a vessel of purity, that is my desire but His supersedes mine. Every mother wants a grandchild but I am not forced—only God gives and I cannot question the maker of the universe. Grandchildren are but a bonus, there are still friends and family members my age or even older who are childless, some say they do not wish to have one and others pray fervently but nothing happens. One thing I know in life is that time and happenstance play a role in our lives; it is not about the willingness nor the resistant but the mercy that we pray to experience. The creator of the universe holds the card; he chooses who to play with and what to incorporate in the game. The fact that you are perchance having fun is not your making, so do not credit yourself, there are those who are making less or no effort but are making it BIG and others who are working so hard like an elephant and eating like an ant. Some are doctorate degree holders but stagnant and others without qualification are making millions. I pray and hope he will find love one day, to marry not to fornicate. I am one of the old schools, bible-believing people that propagate the importance of not having sex before marriage. Excuse me? This is my view and beliefs, not yours, feel free to be yourself while I am unearthing my person to you. At this stage of my son's life some families make ignorant choices like FORCED MARRIAGES, I say no way. Some young ladies cunningly enter households in pretence of loving and caring for your son meanwhile they are looking for immigration stay or a benefactor. My dear, my son has British and American passports, I am not willing to have a girl take advantage of his innocence; I love my son; more so, he is my one and only *kapish* or *capisci* (Italian meaning *understand*). They say love has no boundaries but these days and age people draw boundaries and ensure they have a gain. My dear, I will not have sleepless night or take pain killer over an issue that God himself is determinant factor. Let me ask you sincerely, have worries and anxiety transcended into progress? The more you battle with life, the more you are plagued by your encounter. Do not be delusional as there are things we can never change in life by our own strength, so why are you a slave of anxiety. The maker of the universe understands that there are things beyond human reasoning and anxiety and he said, 'cast all your burdens to me for I care'. Sweetheart, the energy you give to worries is enough to be transferred into life impending accomplishment. Some of us have had heart attacks, strokes, blood pressures, emotional comfort eating leading to weight gain, cancer, and lost their lives due to stress of things what have become us and cannot leave us alone to exist as God has intended. I am taking a deep breath now, because the surge and demand of daily living can take drastic measures or turn. Sometimes it is gradually and others it comes like torrents and you lose control of your emotions. Do not be embittered about the twist and turns of life because the more we get sucked into bitters the worse the bile excretion in our body become, polluting our entire organs and systems. I am a firm believer of tomorrow and the possibility of change that might come with the dawn.

Weeping may endure for a night but joy comes in the morning

CHAPTER 24

Tony's Mum

I have told you a lot about Tony all this while but this time I will tell you about myself and what kept me and how I have been kept. My life has been a turbulent one from onset but my creator has always calmed the storm of my life. There have been various floods that nearly drowned my destiny but they stood still. I have had to encounter various mountains on my way to the goal, even though they made my mission impossible but they became a plain. There are many more stories of my life I would have kept telling you. But be rest assured that my creator does not do things halfway, what He starts he brings to completion. He has made me step into impossibility and have climaxed into success. I have walked in the shoes of legends and tread the path of the rich and famous. People have been forced to show me favour and I have been forced to show people favour. I travelled the path of the unknown and have ended with much knowledge. The epic of my existence is insurmountable and my plight is that I can never ever thank my creator enough. I have experienced those who show me kindness, experience the goodness in the land of the living and the wicked ones go through life wondering what is going on. I have been through heart breaks and disappointments yet I stand tall in every life cross examination. I have over the years become the prosecutor of life trial trying to make sense of all my short comings.

I have been trying to identify the key players of existence especially my life, it has proven impossible. I am glad that I am not one of those women parading themselves as cupid best mate. I am far from it; perhaps if I was given a chance in love, I would have embraced it with humility. Unfortunately, men are looking for women that have no added burden like a child with disability as far as I am concerned it is their lose because we are created with big heart and lots of love to give that is why we are entrusted to care for special children with an unflinching love, care and affection

Where were you?

Where were you

When I had to keep awake

Even when my eyes were heavy with sleep

Where were you when I had to mop the floor?

Endlessly but tirelessly

When I had to clean even in sickness

When I had to provide even in lack

Where were you

When all hope seems to be lost

And a divine intervention showed up

Where were you, when I had to drag myself up

To take care of my children, even in pain and sickness

Where were you, when I had to toil and flood my being with sweat?
Where were you, when I had to, even if I could not push myself any
further?

Where were you, when I, alone took the deep plunge?

Where were you, when I had to cry myself to sleep?

Where were you, when I need comfort and a shoulder to lean on?

But divine intervention cuddled me to his bosom

Where were you when I was all alone?

With no friends and family

Even when life issues were almost drowning me

Yet I had to keep my head high above sea level

and my chin, just on top of the surface.

And my eyes wide open

Where were you, when I had to fix my life regardless of the mess?

And I made a message out of the mess

Where were you, when life was full of impossibilities and mishaps?

In these entire Crisis you never showed up

But Christ walked in and overturned the situation

Where were you when I had to crawl to clean my house?

Where were you when life drama preamble took a negative turn?

Perhaps you were dinning and winning

Or binging gluttonously on lust

Maybe scavenging in obscenity and lasciviousness

And now you walk into my life like a god

Parading yourself in egocentric emptiness

And now you want me to fend for you

Excuse me!!!!!!

CHAPTER 25

My Sacrifices

How did I do all these you might wonder? It came with lots of sacrifices and self-denial. I have always worked part-time from the time the kids were younger. I earned less but gained more satisfaction from my role as a mother. I saw the children grow from strength to strength and I played the entire role. I learnt a lot from the kids and they taught me one or two things I also impacted them one way or the other. I dedicated time and money to ensure my daughter was up to scratch. I enjoyed parenting my children and especially my son, it built a lot of resilience in me and restructured my personality. Due to the fact that I was working part-time I decided to engage in voluntary sectors in order to build my skills and it did help. I acquired experiences in board room, social service sector, schools, and church. I studied any professional course that was marketable at that minute. I did computer science, even created programmes, was unable to continue in information technology sector despite the money due to lack of flexibility of the sector. I Left and went to study law, I managed to gain experiences and refused to be debarred by my care limitations or allow my expectations to be cut short. I even sacrificed my privacy; we all slept in one family size bed when they were children in order to keep an eye on Tony. I spent half of the night praying and submitting myself to divine direction. I stopped visiting friends as I would not want to pose any difficulty for people who might keep asking my son 'don't touch', 'keep it', 'sit down', and 'stop it'. To avoid all these it is best to become not to socialise than socialise and get yourself insulted or your child abused? I could not sleep unless Tony falls asleep; I became more like human computer and time *tick-tock-tick-tock*. At work I had to work extra and became the best at work, I worked hard to make up for my absence due to demand from Tony's school. I had to monitor his movement like a hawk. It is a noble role but it mobilises you psychologically and mentally. Tony is a success story and his journey is not just one off but there are many others who have embarked or are embarking in similar journey and I wish you all the best. I sometimes had to vacuum clean the floor over three times a day though he can clean it if I ask him to, but sometimes I am too tired to request for help. I also spend money on food he eats and eats like a horse and always buy organic to curb hyperactive behaviour. I am enjoying the person I have become or who Tony has conditioned me to be perhaps I may not be able to achieve all these if not for the challenges posed by autism. After eleven years of working in the public sector I took a voluntary redundancy to care for my son and become self-employed and own my company. I needed to go, it has been a hectic journey and my role at work is vey tasking. Most importantly, I put a smile on my children's faces because when they are leaving mum is at home and when they are back here I am waiting to take care of them. Being a mum is a very rewarding role and I wish every mother reading this divine wisdom because that is all you need to embark on this journey. Some have tried but failed and others have been very successful. I pray that you will succeed and become a success story.

Hard Truth about life

Many started this journey with their children being diagnosed with autism. Some children have moved on and became university undergraduates, some at colleges doing mainstream courses, others in special needs schools thriving and have very good communication skills with poor social skill. Others have not achieved quite but managing in making few sentences when prompted. There are others who are mute and cannot utter a vowel or an alphabet. These are all very different situations created by autism. Some of them who have and are achieving are having very challenging behaviour as their mental ability is challenging life realities as the way they see life is very different. While others with complex learning difficulties cannot make sense of the mumbo jumbo of life. They see life as nonsensical and meaningless. The family life has become very demanding for most and for others it is of no concern; the journey is filled with support, empowerment, and encouragement. On the other hand, there are families who have lost the will to live and have purchased hopelessness in the hands of the uncanny distributor. No matter where you are at, and where you ought to be, just take it one prayerful, hopeful day at a time.

Recap of the Moment

Tony is still diagnosed with autism so to speak almost 20 years later, sill counting but I have not lost count of the grace that has sustained us as a family and still awaiting for a spiritual revamping of all the works of autism. There is progress and I celebrate it with full gratitude to almighty God. It might seem bleak at this minute but I can see a glimpse of light at the other end of my anxiety. It might seem helpless but I know that help has already come perhaps I fail to grasp the momentum of the moment. I am hoping in the midst of hopelessness that my situation will give birth to a celebration. I have looked around and have searched all corners of human existence available to me to investigate on, and I have come to the conclusion that I really have no say. I can only do the best I can to assist and support Tony to cope with life demands ensuring that life does not pull a trigger of delusional disorder where the reality of life is farfetched. I would, at this point, commend life as it is rather unbecoming to alleviate myself to accept life trophy dropped indiscriminately on my lap. I am unique to be equipped to handle an uncommon family problem with all life assistance at my command, so to speak, ironically. I still feel lonely as no one can understand deeply my situation. Some might empathise but empathy is not as deep as visualising a circumstance, as autism affects all aspects of the family well-being. Every child is unique; it is rare to equate similar characteristics to every person. So are parents of these children, they come in unique sachet deflector unrecognised and unused. I call myself Iron Lady because I am coping, not by my strength or ability but an inward existence of unending victory. Everyone sees me as having no issues but to observers its mere exaggeration and drama, with me and Tony as casts taking on main role. The secret is that I have managed my time effectively regardless of what life is exhibiting. Time is a big thing, it needs to be managed properly, every second every minute matters. Time is something you can never get back but can lose. Time is a powerful element in human existence and can, within a second, enrich the impoverished. Wisdom is another one, get wisdom and you will be swimming in self-actualisation. Another party to all the facts of life is organisation, if life is blowing horns of unsettlement then you need to pop out your skills and settle life issues by getting yourself organised, like the popular saying 'the devil is in the detail'.

Life inevitable situations are organised before they encroach your privacy otherwise it will be impossible for them to gain entry. I may, at this minute, seem or look confused I must confess I am on top of the game, when life has refused me rest then I will ensure that neither I nor life will have a peaceful moment to meditate on life. You need to ensure you keep healthy, eat well and sleep well, ensure you have respite where you chill and deflect life issues. I hate crowd and outing that makes me exert too much energy, I enjoy watching movies, holidays, music and any activity that will engulf and engage my entire being solemnity. Stress should not be encouraged our life as it is, is stressful enough, why don't you put your feet up, relax and accommodate the reality of life gestures as your worries cannot conquer the inevitable. The more you worry the more your health is in jeopardy, thrive, make it work for you regardless of what is on the table. I may see my son as a king in the making or a future president. You might see him as a non-entity or never do well. Regardless of what both opinions are we have to latch onto the fact that our opinion is irrelevant and cannot eschew life pronouncement but will aid my daily optimistic outlook on life. You cannot imagine how I feel when I see functioning adults with autism and how life treats them as non-existence. They are being bullied and called names. As I am writing this, I have a young man sitting next to me diagnosed with autism. He came to sit next to me and a young lady, he said hello and I responded but the lady was totally oblivious of his presence. He then asked inappropriately 'what is your name?' Well typical autistic behaviour, I smiled. Thinking Tony might someday find himself in that kind of situation. I love my son to bits and will be unhappy for him to be maltreated so I try to sow a seed of goodness which my son can reap in the future. It is painful to wonder what will happen to the fruit of your womb when you say goodbye to planet earth. How will the planet and its entirety look out for him? That is the bit I worry. We cannot be in this world forever but we pray that the seed we have sown will be harvested by our children. People think that pride and selfishness makes us look great and different. I would rather say it negates our children's future. Show me a just and upright man who is kind and selfless. I will show you a man whose children and children's children are surging in favour. This might not be from people you have been good to but a divine goodness. Your labour of love is not dismissed but used to celebrate your life. Please say a prayer for me if you can . . . because I have paused this minute to say thank God. You might wonder why I should thank God in my situation since there seems to be no supposed improvement. I would say for His grace and protection. I am lavished by favour and famished with the need to please the one and only who has kept me ignited with the recognition of grace. Don't cry for me but be happy for the impossible trend life will turn for Tony. Don't pity me or Tony but take a peep for the last time of a climax of Tony and the lunching of a champion. Life hazard has a way of eliminating traces of suspicion but lures you to ponder on what ifs. What if nothing good comes out of all these, I say, I am like modern Abraham not deviating in my belief knowing full well the Lord will not allow my child whom he has given to me to be slaughtered, but wait patiently for an uncommon replacement of Tony's situation. I am daddy's girl, a similitude of uncommon grace and favour packaged in shabby treasure. The more you look the less you see but the answer lies in dissecting nature's package which Tony is one of those. Please say a prayer, this time make a wish for Tony that the impossible will become possible. Sometimes I step out of the situation like an onlooker to visualise the extent life has paraded itself with so much contempt, compounding its philosophical ideology like a pragmatist awaiting a stage managed U turn.

Grand Finale

Sweetheart, we have just taken a bow and have left the audience in solemnity, confused at what just transpired. To some it may not sound or look real. Some have been taken aback and made positive life changing decisions and others are still sitting on the fence. The cast have been fully staged and the director perhaps pleased with the performance. I, Tony, and Tochi are in the cast submissively taking turns to act in our role as scripted. The observers and spectators are unsure what to expect but as the action continues, they take life notes and tearful glance. Life is a journey that we all have taken and in the process we pray that our expectations will not be cut short. Darling, there are no new challenges on earth, neither are there new heartbreak, all have been experienced. You are not the first neither will you be the last. The tears you shed yesterday for an issue has been shed by millions of others in different parts of the world. I am not the first woman with an autistic son; there are lots of women out there. I am not the only one thriving and making positive impact from the situation, there are thousands of others. If you think you have arrived there are millions of others who got to the destination before you. If you think life challenges have been so demanding there are others with demands placed on them every second. Whilst you are thinking you are complete and there is no lack, there are others much more, but sweetheart, you know this second but the next you don't know. Take a look at all life situations, do checks and balances and the conclusion is you can never have an answer. I can only say, take it one day at a time and lean on your maker for things you don't know and cannot challenge and that is tomorrow, the next second, the next minute, but we are hopeful it turns out good. I pray and hope that you step out of your disheartening situation and step into hope.

The race is not to the swift or the battle to the strong, nor does food come to the wise or wealth to the brilliant or favor to the learned; but time and chance happen to them all.

T

Steps to making positive changes

Your child is not a Monster but needs attention

Taking care of a child with Autism can be demanding both physically, emotionally and psychologically, but we as parents need to realise that our duty to our children is to nurture and protect them from external and internal hazardous stimuli. The more time we take to care and understand our children the less demanding our roles will become. Some of us are painfully subjected to being battered by our children with Autism; this can be very painful and disheartening. We are turn between safeguarding them and living in fear of being injured. The ailment lives everyone bamboozled with no forth coming answers or solution. Some have given up and resorted to putting them in foster care. This not your fault please do not beat yourself, our situations are all very different please do not beat yourself. Our children are all different so are our coping mechanism. You need to understand your child's fear and uncertainty and try to alleviate them. None of us are experts and neither are there professionals who have wealth of knowledge, but playing a guessing game. No research has been conclusive in the issue of autism perhaps we need to conclude that they are just natures differentiations, unique and non-conforming to the theory of human ideology-so what is this ideal? I made a choice to find my answers and in my quest I made some changes which helped me adjust in my role.

I have a 20-year-old son, who was diagnosed with autism at an early age and I raised him up as a single parent after my marital break down. At the age of 15 he started self harming and due to the impact of constantly hitting his ears it became cauliflower shaped. I was working at the time and he was in school and had little time to investigate on what the problem was. It got serious that he was excluded from school and was almost sectioned for self harming. This was rather alarming, as God would have it, I was made redundant from my job of almost 12 years and that was at the time I needed it. It was an opportunity to revisit what has been going on in his life.

- I stopped giving him yogurt every morning, I thought since I am allergic to milk he might be allergic too, so I discontinued yogurt and it reduced.

- I bought sensory lights different types at home; they are not expensive, buy affordable one.

- I started using blackout curtains, tried as much as possible to reduce external environmental overload. It is no longer about getting something fanciful but effective.

- I made sure that the TV volume is right and that what he viewed was appropriate.

- I stopped talking to him or asking him to stop when he is self harming sometimes it could be attention seeking, being stubborn or manipulative. Talking to a child self harming makes it worse.

- I gave him pain killers to avert the impact of the blow

- I stopped making long telephone conversations in front of him

- I stopped giving him Harmonica and keyboard (Instruments like these hurts his ears and his school was giving it to him to pacifier him, but instead it made him worse.)

- Instead he used computer apps to play the instruments

- Sometimes it can be Hormonal, watch the space if your child is going through puberty and in her menstrual cycle, please seek your GP advice on how to minimise the impact of PMS.

- Show and tell your child you love her, even if she is mute that will not debar her understanding.

- You can actually speak to your child when they are calm about the impact of their self harming. Don't worry if they don't respond but they do understand.

- Ensure your child is wearing suitable clothing and they are neither too warm nor too cold and is not hungry, as these can trigger self harming episodes.

- Avoid exposing (Try not to expose) your child to any form of sexualised behaviour particularly what they watch he or she is not able to delete and filter inappropriate information otherwise they will not be diagnosed with Autism.

- Please ensure you establish eye contact in every communication it shows your child that you have time for them and they will always respond positively.

- He suffered badly with PICA and loves eating dry leaves anywhere especially in the garden or growing outside. I decided to give him plant based food instead, like spinach and broccoli. It did minimise it.

- He loves eating tissues so I stopped putting tissue in the toilet and cut some bit whenever he needed to use the toilet and he completely stopped.

It is vital that we keep ourselves sane and our children save. All these measures I mentioned above assisted in giving my son a descent life without putting himself in danger. These children are very loving and caring, remember what you give is what you get. Children with Autism easily form attachment than children without autism. Take out time research, read, explore and it will assist you to combat and manage the ailment effectively.

Teenage and adulthood stage

You should bear in mind that your child though has special needs is still going through adolescence and transitioning into adulthood. We need to learn to respect that, and ensure people around us accord the same respect especially their younger sibling who are cognitively high functioning. I started by giving my son opportunity to make choices as to what he would want or do. I always ask his carers to ask him what he would like to do, like if he would like going out or staying indoors. I noticed that they just ask him to get up and go and when he gets out there he becomes frustrated. He is older now and I need to listen to his opinion, even down to clothing and meal choices. Please understand that all the struggles people raising up children of the same age are bound to experience will not escape him or her so learn to adjust, it will alleviate your struggles. Learn to speak politely, please, sorry and thank you goes a long way, watch the tone of your voice it speaks volumes. Avoid talking about him in front of him, it gets him upset and avoid giving undivided attention by getting consumed in an unending conversation whilst he is there. Autism does not debar hormonal, mind, emotional functions, your child might not say much but he retains a lot which sometimes springs up as self harming episodes. If your child is in her period please learn to study her mood as to see if she suffer from PMS, these might make self harming and violence worse. They feel sorry for themselves sometimes, it is normal to be frustrated by setback in life but we need to jump start their joy of existence.

WHO IS NOT AUTISTIC THESE DAYS (ROBOTECH WORLD)

What is normal and what is not normal? And who determines what is normal? Life is becoming very interesting, people and professionals seem to be looking for signs of abnormality in children. We are living in a microwave age; parents are no longer waiting for their children to reach appropriate milestone but putting them under so much pressure. Parents of children who lack boundaries and control are beginning to resort to labelling to avert their lack of parenting skills.

Who says that a child should speak and walk at a particular age? I am surprised that we all have not learnt our lessons yet, that every child is different and should be given opportunity to develop naturally. We should remember that none of us play a part in the creation process or conception, so we should just watch the developmental stages with the hope that it comes out normal. I see the creator as a perfect master artist endowed with perfection. Where did the imperfection we claim come from? Did it come from our lack of tolerance and patience? How can a high functioning autistic person who is very talented and a genius, claim abnormality, just because they communicate and socialise differently?

There are so many creatures in the universe that are not concerned by the abnormally of life yet they grow unperturbed. Those of us that have Pets have you ever observed an abnormality in our pets, I guess not. At what stage in life does your Dog need to start barking and warding off intruders? How many dogs have labels of developmental delays or is it just a human thing? Who is normal these days when life pressures have taken a toll on human existence, technology have taken over human normal communication and socialisation. How many of our young people really communicate appropriately or socialise appropriately, perhaps that is why anti social behaviour is on the increase.

Who is not Autistic in this present generation when the so called normal has turned into abnormal, even when respected leaders are making decisions that you would under normal circumstance say it is obviously abnormal. I am beginning to think the children tagged with Autism are the normally of life. I am not sure if it has occurred to us that there are people who are meant to be a particular way as long as they do not cause commotion or disrupt others from enjoying their existence. Playing with the mind of the Autistic could it be like performing cosmetic surgery. Most of these children are upset when you interrupt their quiet times alone. Have you considered why these kids are geniuses? They spend most of their time in solemnity and soberness making them capable to engage their mind to exploration.

The famous Physicist Albert Einstein was born in 1879, not at the time of Autistic Labelling, I am sure he would have been diagnosed with Autism in the 21st century. Travelling back in time he was very smart intellectually and socially perhaps isolated, who cared then. Looking at his quote one would understand that despite his theoretical ingenuity he was still flabbergasted by the creation process and human existence. If you begin to dissect the intricacy of existence you will definitely go bonkers. The normal are yet to be born in the definition man has given to normality.

'Two things are infinite: the universe and human stupidity; and I'm not sure about the universe. The most beautiful thing we can experience is the mysterious. It is the source of all true art and science'. Albert Einstein.

The world is crazy and people in it are full of weird behaviour, the computer is taking over the mind of man and his thinking faculty. In due season human beings will start cloning geniuses with autism to carry out delicate complicated programs. We are opportune to have nature's unique personality in our care to care for, why do you need to change them to be what they are not meant to be. They have the ability to thrive even better and more brilliantly than most if you give them time. Labelling has taken over our parental duties, long suffering and resilience that is why, we have resorted to pampering and managing our children. I have to tell you that your child can do most things if you let them unless they are mentally retarded or have fragile X perhaps have psychopathic tendency. Autism, ADHD and dyslexia are becoming the latest excuses for laziness and sloppiness As our society is cuddling up to labelling some people are taking advantage to avoid some of the regular things they need to do. When they are behind their mates academically, they receive a label. When they are badly behaved, they receive a label. One of the ways I have groomed my son into being independent by giving him the key to the house even though I will be at home. He opens the door lets himself in, locks the door behind him put the chain on. He will then warm his food and sit down to eat and get himself a drink. If he needs bread he can toast the bread and butter it. The maker of the universe does not make mistakes neither does he regret his creativity. He displays them in life gallery and parades them with so much pride and grace. Do complete self -awakening test of why you do what you do? We are creatures of habits and passion which makes us mortal, we have the ability to copy and please others without thinking about what we really want. Why does your child's ability panic you? Is it because of people and how they perceive you and your family? My dear, that is low self esteem, take the first step by accepting your child's situation and work to improve and get them better rather than manage them the way they are. Your parental role is to enable, promote, and encourage change, please try, and give your child a chance. Nature is waiting to inscribe them in the wall of fame, if you let them be who they are meant to be. The world is also ready to celebrate their uniqueness if you let them be. I will tell you a short story about my friend Helena which I titled limitless.

Limitless

I will invite you to read about my friend Helena and her son Robert. He was my son's very good friend when they were growing up. He was very rough and disruptive that his mum was always sceptical about taking him to anywhere. The first time he visited me he broke my Television set, I did not mind because I understood his situation. Due to the fact his mum had always kept him under lock and key due to his behaviour hence he struggled to cope outside the home environment and got too excited if he had to go out. I encouraged mum to keep taking him out and treating him like every other child. We went through a lot together, we visited nutritionists and we were given vitamins and supplements for the children. We sought all manner of help to get our children to function the way we felt was normal. He got potty trained before Tony and went to mainstream, whilst Tony went to special needs school as he was not potty trained. As time went on Tony improved in Primary school and thrived. When he got to the age of 13 Tony regressed whilst he progressed into mainstream secondary school. He started doing very well and made As' in all his papers in GCSE, from there he was taken in the same school to do

A levels and he got A* in all his papers. So to speak he is in University though diagnosed with Autism still have so called abnormal social and communication skills. My situation was very different; she had a supportive husband who was ready to work with her and bring about change in their son. Do you have such support? On my part I had an absent father who was not ready to support us. My emotions took the best of me and I had another child. My friend had only her son and can concentrate all her energy on him. Don't beat yourself life is too short and we are all very different and so are our circumstances. Use all you can available to you to change what you need to change. What is important to you, the cognitive or the social skills you decide? The high can be reached with any means possible so why don't you avail yourself of all the resources possible to assist your child get there? I rest my case whilst I live you to ponder on all the eventualities of life, whilst I close the chapters and bid you farewell.

Printed in Great Britain
by Amazon